T0356720

THE
WRITER'S
LOT

THE
WRITER'S
LOT

*Culture and Revolution
in Eighteenth-Century France*

ROBERT DARNTON

THE BELKNAP PRESS OF
HARVARD UNIVERSITY PRESS
Cambridge, Massachusetts
London, England
2025

Printed in the United States of America
First printing

Library of Congress Cataloging-in-Publication Data

Names: Darnton, Robert, author.
Title: The writer's lot : culture and revolution in eighteenth-century France /
Robert Darnton.
Description: Cambridge, Massachusetts : The Belknap Press of Harvard
University Press, 2025. | Includes bibliographical references and index.
Identifiers: LCCN 2024049812 (print) | LCCN 2024049813 (ebook) |
ISBN 9780674299887 (cloth) | ISBN 9780674300637 (pdf) |
ISBN 9780674300644 (epub)
Subjects: LCSH: French literature—18th century—History and criticism. |
Literature and society—France—History—18th century. | Books and reading—
France—History—18th century. | France—Intellectual life—18th century. |
LCGFT: Literary criticism.
Classification: LCC PQ261 .D36 2025 (print) | LCC PQ261 (ebook) |
DDC 840.9/005—dc23/eng/20241104
LC record available at https://lccn.loc.gov/2024049812
LC ebook record available at https://lccn.loc.gov/2024049813

CONTENTS

THE
WRITER'S
LOT

INTRODUCTION

Paths to Grub Street

I N FEBRUARY 2024, the Institute for Advanced Studies in Paris invited me to spend a month on an intriguing assignment: self-criticism. I was to look back over my early work and to reconsider some arguments that have become absorbed in the current understanding of eighteenth-century French history.

I chose an article published in 1971, "The High Enlightenment and the Low-Life of Literature in Pre-Revolutionary France."[1] It provoked considerable debate when it first appeared. Since then it has been accepted, even by its critics, as a work that occupies a central place in histories of the origins of the French Revolution.[2] Now, more than fifty years later, it needs to be revised.

In the article, I argued that historians and literary scholars had failed to take account of an important sector of the literary world, which I called "Grub Street," drawing on a parallel with London, where hack writers lived down and out in a street of that name during the seventeenth century. They scattered to garrets in other locations throughout the city in the eighteenth century. But a periodical, *The Grub Street Journal* (1730–1738), made the name stick as a pejorative for hacks, and Alexander Pope, who contributed to the journal, pilloried them in *The Dunciad* (three versions, 1728 to 1743). No such street existed in Paris, but scribblers proliferated there, too, churning out hack work and living miserably in garrets.

Having studied the career of one of them, Jacques-Pierre Brissot, a future leader of the Girondists during the French Revolution, and having run across many others in the archives of the police, I became convinced that they constituted a distinct milieu with a subculture of its own. As many identified with Jean-Jacques Rousseau, they eventually came to be known as "les Rousseau du ruisseau" (Rousseaus of the gutter). Yet they admired Voltaire and aspired to win fame as philosophes by following his example. When they knocked on the door of his "church," however, it remained closed. Paris was flooded with aspiring writers in the 1770s and 1780s, and there was no room for them in the system of patronage and clientelism, which formed the basis of most literary careers.

To be sure, a few made it to the top, but they belonged to the second generation of philosophes—men like Jean-Baptiste-Antoine Suard and Jean-François Marmontel, who, unlike their predecessors, did not face serious persecution, though they spent a brief time in the Bastille—and settled comfortably into the salons and academies, where the plumbs were passed around. By the beginning of the reign of Louis XVI in 1774, the state permitted most philosophical works to circulate freely, unlike the 1750s, when the *Encyclopédie* was banned and most Encyclopedists—with the exception of a few stalwarts led by Diderot, who was secretly protected by Lamoignon de Malesherbes, the head administrator of the book trade—ran for cover and did not emerge until the danger had passed. I described the 1770s and 1780s as the period of the "High Enlightenment" in contrast to the "heroic" Enlightenment of the midcentury years. The writers who made it to the top during the last decades of the ancien régime advocated moderate change in the manner of Voltaire while they dominated the Académie française and monopolized pensions and sinecures.

Those at the bottom wallowed in misery. They vented their frustrated ambitions in much of their writing—illegal works, which constituted the most dangerous branch of the book trade, known among booksellers as "livres philosophiques." This literature included some serious philosophy, atheistic works like *Système de la nature*, but it consisted mainly of libels, pornography, and seditious political tracts, which sold in the sector where the risks and profits were greatest. Driven by poverty, the Grub Steet writers attempted to cash in on the demand for scandalous accounts of the private lives of public figures. Such genres did not lend themselves to the exposition of philosophy, but they abounded in anecdotes that conveyed the themes of decadence and despotism. They were seditious in tone rather than logic. Instead of scoring hits with Voltairean wit, Grub Street writers blasted at their targets—the grandees of the court, government, and high society (*le monde*)—with a rhetoric of denunciation and moralizing.[3]

Insofar as they evoked philosophers, the hacks favored Rousseau rather than Voltaire, because Rousseau had turned against the established elite of *le monde*, whereas Voltaire had appealed to it. Yet the hack writers did not renounce the values and ideas championed by the philosophes, nor did they develop ideas of their own. The ideological divide ran along a fault line that was social rather than philosophical. It expressed a contradiction within the Republic of Letters, a realm that supposedly was open to everyone but excluded an increasingly large number of aspirants. The favored few in the second generation of philosophes were integrated in the power structure of the ancien régime and did not challenge its fundamental principles, while the hacks of Grub Street made the entire system look bad. Writers who had suffered from exclusion under the Old Regime of letters—men like Brissot, Marat, and Hébert—expressed a spirit of sedition in language that would resonate among the Jacobins and sans-culottes.

Having accepted the invitation to criticize my own work, I should explain the context in which I wrote "The High Enlightenment and the Low-Life of Literature." In 1968, I belonged to the radical Left that opposed the American intervention in Vietnam, took to the streets after the assassination of Martin Luther King, Jr., and supported student protests from Berkeley to Paris. As a graduate student in Oxford from 1960–1964, I fell under the spell of historians like E. P. Thompson and my supervisor, Richard Cobb, who advocated studying history "from below." After completing my doctorate, I had a brief career as a reporter at *The New York Times*, mainly covering crime. I had been broken in as a reporter for the Newark *Star Ledger*, working from police headquarters in Newark, New Jersey. As I came from a family of newspaper people, I felt sympathy for the "shoe leather" men who saw the world from street level and conveyed their view in clear, clipped prose. For me, the ideal type was Meyer ("Mike") Berger, a veteran crime reporter and friend of my parents, who captured the lives of ordinary people in "About New York," a column for *The Times*.

My critics have taken this sympathy for newspaper work as a symptom of a populist or even an anti-intellectual outlook. I failed to discuss the ideas of the French philosophes in depth, they objected, and I did not provide an adequate interpretation of the Enlightenment.[4] In my view, that indictment, a central theme in a volume about my work entitled *The Darnton Debate*, was unfair, because I never pretended to write a history of the Enlightenment. I had studied the works of the philosophes intensely with one of my tutors at Oxford, Robert Shackleton, an expert on Montesquieu, and before that I spent most of my last semester as an undergraduate dissecting Immanuel Kant's *Critique of Pure Reason*. Later, in doing research on books as items in commercial exchanges, I did not think I was denying their power as vehicles of ideas. I thought I was contributing to something distinct from standard Enlightenment studies: the history of books as a new discipline.

In retrospect, however, I believe my critics scored some valid points. There is an aggressive, anti-elitist tone to my early writing, as if at times I were a sixty-eighter, protesting in the streets. I seemed to sympathize with the hacks of Grub Street and to share their hostility to the literary elite. In my original article about Brissot, published in 1968, I drew on the manuscript papers of Jean-Charles-Pierre Lenoir, the lieutenant general of police in Paris in 1774–1775 and in 1776–1785, which revealed that Brissot had been a paid spy for the police after being released from the Bastille, where he was imprisoned in 1784 under suspicion of collaborating with libelers. I found Lenoir's statement convincing, despite his evident bias. (He wrote it after fleeing from the Revolution, when he had no love for revolutionaries.) Others have contested my interpretation, although they have provided no evidence to disprove Lenoir's remark.[5] I don't believe they have demonstrated their case, but I cringe when I read parts of my own argument, such as the following on Brissot as a police spy:

> The story of his spying deserves emphasis, not in order to pass judgment on Brissot, but in order to understand him. His *embastillement* did not prove the purity of his patriotism, as he argued later. It corrupted him, and in the corrupting it confirmed his hatred of the Old Regime. How he must have hated it! How he must have raged inwardly against the system of arbitrary power that first struck him down and then enlisted him in its service. How he must have reviled the men in control of the system, who first blocked his attempts to win honor for himself and then dishonored him by making him their agent.[6]

If I could expunge anything from my early publications, I would delete those "must haves." How can I know what Brissot must have thought and felt? In speculating about Brissot's inner life, I went beyond the bounds of the evidence and indulged in gratuitous psychologizing. Perhaps for reasons buried in my own biography I identified with Brissot. I have written a 500-page draft of a biography of him and left it in a filing cabinet as if it were a part of my early life that I would prefer to keep private.

The subjective element in writing history shows through other passages in my descriptions of Grub Street in the 1971 article. For example,

> Is it surprising that the writers whom Voltaire scorned as *la canaille de la littérature* (the scum of literature) should have moralized in the manner of Rousseau in their politico-pornography? To them the Old Regime was obscene. In making them its spies and smut-peddlers, it had violated their moral core and desecrated their youthful visions of serving humanity honorably in Voltaire's church. So they became rank atheists and poured out their souls in blasphemies about the society that had driven them down into an underworld of criminals and deviants.[7]

In rereading that today, it seems overblown and underdocumented. I also find the conclusion of the article too strong, both in its language and in its claim to identify "authentic" radicalism on the eve of the Revolution:

> The crude pamphleteering of Grub Street was revolutionary in feeling as well as in message. It expressed the passion of men who hated the Old Regime in their guts, who ached with the hatred of it. It was from such visceral hatred, not from the refined abstractions of the contented cultural elite, that the extreme Jacobin revolution found its authentic voice.[8]

Aside from the subjective and time-bound character of the argument, the energy behind it came from a more decisive factor: the excitement of coming up with a new idea and the temptation to push it as far as it would go. In 1971, historians generally assumed that a causal link connected the Enlightenment with the Revolution, although they never managed to show how it operated. For my part, I did not deny the influence of the philosophes after 1789, because the revolutionaries often quoted them (Montesquieu as frequently as Rousseau), along with other sources, particularly authors from antiquity.[9] But I believed that enlightened ideas and values had been absorbed in the upper ranks of French society and even in the governing elite before 1789. Despite their differences, Turgot, Necker, Calonne, Brienne, and other ministers of Louis XVI held enlightened views. Some of them intervened to support Charles-Joseph Panckoucke, the publisher who produced many works of the High Enlightenment, including the quarto edition of the *Encyclopédie* and the *Encyclopédie méthodique*. The diffusion of those works did not threaten to topple the power structure. Had there been no crippling royal debt, no disastrous increases in the price of bread, no intransigent opposition by the parlements (sovereign law courts), no incompetent management by the Crown, France might have ridden out the crises that brought down the ancien régime.

To be sure, this string of "might haves" looks as tenuous as the "must haves" that I just disavowed. Yet the more I study the course of events between 1750 and 1800, the more importance I attribute to contingency, unforeseen consequences, miscalculation, and sheer accident, such as the hailstorm in the Paris region of July 13, 1788. I am not persuaded by historians who argue that some form of Enlightenment discourse brought down the ancien régime and determined the course of the Revolution.[10] Insofar as the regime was vulnerable to ideological disruption, I still believe that my argument from 1971 is valid. The political system could assimilate Enlightenment principles and even profit from applying them—that is, by promoting greater equality in the collection of taxes and the administration of justice, as well as specific measures such as the abolition of the *corvée* (forced labor in road building), the withdrawal of internal custom duties, and toleration of Protestants.

The government enacted some of these reforms and attempted to do more in 1787–1788, when it was blocked by the parlements and surges of hostile public opinion. The parlements were aristocratic bodies, whose members usually sided with the enemies of the Revolution after 1788. But they commanded widespread support during the prerevolutionary crisis, when large crowds took to the streets and rioted in order to block what they perceived as ministerial despotism. That perception did not derive directly from the Enlightenment, although it was compatible with some works of the philosophes, especially *De l'Esprit des lois*. It developed over decades of protests and pamphleteering about abuses of power and decadence among the governing elite.[11]

Those themes went back to the Mazarinades of the Fronde and the Phillipiques of the Regency. As the names suggest, they were personal attacks on men in power (Cardinal Jules Mazarin and the Regent, Phillipe, duke of Orléans), and they were followed by powerful barrages at the end of the regime: the Maupeouana of 1771–1775 directed against Chancellor René Nicolas de Maupeou and the Calonniana of 1787, which helped bring down controller general Charles Alexandre de Calonne. Libeling was a major industry in Grub Street. Far from expounding abstract ideas, it stirred passions, operating at street level among ordinary Frenchmen. In retrospect, I concede that I overstated my Grub Street argument, but I believe it uncovered an unknown aspect of the Revolution's ideological origins.

In order to trace ideological currents, I spent most of the years after 1971 studying the diffusion of books. The archives of the Société typographique de Neuchâtel supplemented by French sources, especially the papers of the Bastille, made it possible to identify the "livres philosophiques" and to show how they penetrated into the social order of the ancien régime. In fact, I concentrated so heavily on this theme that I became identified with it—at least to one French historian who located me in the eighteenth century: "One of the main producers of the seditious works was a certain Robert Darnton, a publisher in Thionville. He worked with the Société typographique de Neuchâtel, which printed scandalous gazettes and pamphlets. To camouflage this criminal activity, Darnton also published, quite legally, almanacs, pious books and scholarly works."[12]

I found the history of books so intriguing as a new discipline that I suspended my research on authors and concentrated on subjects such as printing, pirating, censorship, bookselling, and the politics of publishing, which concerned books in general, including legal works and the *Encyclopédie*. Yet I continued to think of prerevolutionary France as vulnerable to two tendencies that had escaped previous research: the expansion of a particular sector of the book trade, "livres philosophiques," and the growth of a particular social milieu, Grub Street. They did not always converge (some illegal books were written by respectable authors, and some hack writers produced inoffensive works), but they coincided often enough to undermine the political system's legitimacy.

In my current research, I have returned to the theme of authorship, and by doing so intend to close a cycle that opened up more than fifty years ago. I also hope to correct my original argument by confronting two main objections.

First, taken as a social reality rather than a metonym, Grub Street may have been relatively unimportant. How many writers actually occupied the bottom ranks of the literary world? Did their number increase during the eighteenth century? And if the population grew, did it create the kind of pressure that can be associated with an alienated intelligentsia? Although those questions involve sociological theory—from Vilfredo Pareto to Pierre Bourdieu—they are empirical in nature and can be answered, at least approximately.

Second, hack writing did not necessarily lead to Jacobinism. Hacks produced propaganda for anyone who would pay them, including government ministers before 1789 and, at least in a few cases, counterrevolutionary interests afterward.[13] Moreover, Jacobinism derived from many sources, some of them unrelated to the conditions of life at the bottom of the literary world, and what I have characterized as Grub Street literature did not always come from Grub Street. Libels sometimes were produced by writers located further up in the social order, and the notion of Grub Street itself ("basse littérature" or "littérature des bas-fonds" in French) could have been primarily a fiction, used polemically by some writers to vilify their enemies.

This book provides well-documented estimates of the literary population during the second half of the eighteenth century. Although they demonstrate that the number of writers had at least doubled between 1750 and 1789, they do not show what proportion of the total was made up by scribblers who had no fixed income or employment. *Le Petit Almanach de nos grands hommes* lists 672 obscure poets in 1788, and I have checked enough of its references to verify their accuracy. But it says nothing about their financial situation. A survey of writers living in Paris between 1748 and 1752 by Joseph d'Hémery, the police inspector for the book trade, mentions many impoverished hacks among the 500 he identified. For example,

> AUBLET de Maubuy: He is a young man who has lost his mother and father and who at first was an abbé, then a clerk of an attorney, and finally without an occupation. He lived in a boarding house while seeking a job and seemed to need one very badly. He is clever, writes verse and many satires, both against the clergy and against the Parlement, which he has printed by Beauvais, where he often goes for supper.[14]

Yet d'Hémery left many blank spaces in his reports, and one cannot assume that the authors whose occupations were not identified, even those "without an occupation," were starving scribblers. True, the number of cases like Aublet probably increased along with the total number of writers from 1750 to 1789. Pierre-Jean Audouin, a future Jacobin, typifies these hacks as they appeared in police reports from the 1780s:

> AUDOUIN, calls himself a lawyer, writes manuscript newsletters, peddles forbidden books. He is connected with

Prudhomme, Manuel, and other disreputable authors and peddlers. He does all sorts of jobs; he will be a spy if one wants.[15]

The proportion of such "pauvres diables" (poor devils) within the literary population probably increased, because the prestige of writers, especially celebrities like Voltaire and Rousseau, attracted an increasingly large number of aspirants to literary glory during the last three decades of the ancien régime. But no hard data support these "probablies." They derive from literary sources like *Le Petit Almanach*, Louis-Sébastien Mercier's *Tableau de Paris*, and more obscure works such as Simon-Nicolas-Henri Linguet's *L'Aveu sincère, ou lettre à une mère sur les dangers que court la jeunesse en se livrant à un goût trop vif pour la littérature* (Sincere confession, or letter to a mother about the dangers encountered by youth in giving itself over to too strong a taste for literature).

The literary character of the sources does not mean, however, that they were sheer fiction, divorced from social reality. *Le Neveu de Rameau* (Rameau's nephew) for example, contains a vivid portrait of a hack, who lives on the fringes of the established world of musicians and artists:

His first concern when he gets up in the morning is to know where he will dine. After dinner he thinks about where he will go for supper. Night time also brings worries. Either he will return on foot to a small attic he inhabits—unless his landlady, tired of waiting for the rent, has demanded the return of its key—or else he takes refuge in a tavern on the outskirts of the city, where he whiles away the night with a piece of bread and a tankard of wine.[16]

Far from being a figment of Diderot's imagination, the nephew actually existed, living in Grub Street. He published his own description of his lot in a long poem, *La Rameïde*:

> Quoique j'aie tenu la route peu commune,
> Ce ne fut point pour moi, celle de la fortune.
> (Although I did not follow the common path,
> That was not the one that led to wealth.)[17]

Diderot worked the description of the nephew's miserable, marginal existence into philosophical reflections on the nature of morality and the self—including Diderot's own self (the "MOI" of the dialogue), for he, too, had lived in Grub Street. So had his friend from the 1740s, Jean-Jacques Rousseau, a vagabond and an impoverished musician who probably served as a model for the nephew, at least in part— that is, the part that characterized deviant genius.

Voltaire frequently derided his enemies as literary hacks, desperate to scratch up a few *sous*. His satire, *Le Pauvre Diable*, corresponded closely to the experience of actual writers. In reconstructing the biography of one of them, the abbé Le Senne, a scribbler so obscure that his first name remains unknown, I tried to show how the downward trajectory of a career fit the pattern sketched by Voltaire.[18] My purpose was not to treat literature as a source for social history but rather to draw on fiction as a way to understand the inner lives of the writers I studied.

In reassessing my earlier views, I am still convinced that frustrated ambition existed everywhere in the lower ranks of the literary world, although I consider it as only one of many elements in the collective consciousness of authors. It certainly fueled several revolutionary careers, particularly among marginal writers, because they confronted a contradiction that ran through every sector of literary life under the ancien régime: in principle the Republic of Letters was open equally to everyone and success was earned by talent; in practice, it was a closed world dominated by patronage and privilege. A brief look at some careers shows how this contradiction was experienced and expressed (or elided) among writers who became radical Jacobins.

Fabre d'Églantine figures in the police reports as a typical hack: "A mediocre poet who drags about in shame and poverty. He is despised everywhere. Among men of letters he is considered an execrable subject."[19] As explained in chapter 3, his play, *Les Gens de lettres* (1787), builds its plot around the theme of the barriers to the recognition of genius. Yet this indictment of the world of letters is an exception in Fabre's early writing. His previous plays read like those of other minor authors, and his career conformed to a pattern set by playwrights in the seventeenth century.[20] Like Molière, he bounced around the provinces with itinerant troupes for many years before attempting to conquer Paris. His published work, from *Laure et Pétrarque* (1780), a comic opera, to *Augusta* (1787), a five-act tragedy, dealt with standard themes, without a hint of seditious sentiment. None succeeded on the stage, and all were soon forgotten, although Fabre managed to get them published—without running into difficulties with the censors and police. After finally scoring a hit with *Le Philinte de Molière* (1790), he wrote a few more plays but ceased to depend on the theater as a source of income. The Revolution offered him the opportunity of a new career as a political activist, and he seized it.

Other future Jacobins also struggled in vain to make a name for themselves as authors before the Revolution, writing in a conventional manner without showing symptoms of radicalism. Like Fabre d'Églantine, Jean-Marie Collot d'Herbois spent his youth as an itinerant actor and playwright, and the plays he wrote conformed to the standard formulas of light comedy and the *drame bourgeois*. In *Lucie, ou les parents imprudents* (1781), young lovers overcome the opposition of narrow-minded parents in a plot that could have come from Molière, although it has none of his wit. *Le Paysan magistrat* (1780) contains a few passages that challenge aristocratic privilege, but it is set safely in Spain, and love triumphs in the end, leaving the social order undisturbed.[21]

Jacques-Nicolas Billaud-Varenne, Collot's closest ally in the Committee of Public Safety during the Terror, joined his father's law practice in La Rochelle in 1778, but he attempted to break into the ranks of writers with a play, *La Femme comme il n'y en a plus* (The woman of a kind that is no more). It flopped so badly that Billaud earned a reputation as an all-around failure:

> Désertant le barreau qui n'y perd pas grand'chose,
> Billaud crut chez Thalie avoir plus de succès;
> Mais, auteur sans talents, avocat sans procès,
> Quel fruit a-t-il tiré de sa métamorphose?[22]

> (Deserting the bar, which suffered no great loss,
> Billaud thought he would have more success in the theater,
> But an author without talent and a lawyer without cases,
> What did he gain by his metamorphosis?)

He then took up a garret existence in Paris, supported by odd jobs for lawyers and occasional sums sent by his father.

When money ran out, he fell back on teaching in an Oratorian *collège*, while continuing to write plays. He failed to get them accepted by any Parisian troupe and finally, with an allowance from his father, got inscribed as a lawyer in the Parisian bar. By 1789, he was married, making a modest living, and had turned to political polemics. Two ambitious tracts, published in 1789 but written earlier, showed him to be an enemy of monasticism and a supporter of the Parisian Parlement as a bulwark against ministerial despotism.[23] They contained standard arguments advanced by "patriots" but none of the vitriol that later appeared in the rhetoric of the extreme Left.

The most vitriolic of the future leftists, Jacques-René Hébert, had the most miserable existence as a failed playwright before the Revolution. None of his plays has survived, and little is known about how he supported himself after being condemned for writing a libel while a law clerk in Boissy, Normandy. He fled to Paris and churned out poems and plays, sinking deeper and deeper into poverty. Instead of getting works performed, he managed only to earn a pittance as a ticket collector. During the Terror, Camille Desmoulins tried to undercut Hébert's influence by deriding him as a "collector of tickets" and a sycophant who "opened the loges for aristocrats, bowing down as far as the ground."[24]

Desmoulins himself suffered from poverty as a pamphleteer before the Revolution. Although he joined the Paris bar in 1785, his stutter prevented him from succeeding as a lawyer. He survived by doing clerical work for attorneys and extracting a few louis from his father when he could no longer keep the wolf from the door. He did not qualify to join the National Guard in 1789, because he had no fixed residence. He had been living in one furnished room after another for the last six years, he wrote to his father in October, 1789; and despite the success of his recent pamphlets (*Discours de la lanterne aux Parisiens* and *La France libre*, which were far more radical than Hébert's early works) he was desperate for help. "Would you be so cruel as to refuse me a bed, a pair of sheets?"[25] he asked his father. Desmoulin's journal, *Révolutions de France et de Brabant*, founded in November 1789, finally produced enough income to rescue him from indigence and to launch his career as a politician.

Another friend of Desmoulins, Louis-Antoine de Saint-Just, serves as a final example of the most radical Jacobins, although he did not have much of a prerevolutionary career, because he was only twenty-two when the Bastille was stormed. Still, he wrote a one-act play, *Arlequin-Diogène*, in 1789. It features Harlequin, the favorite character of boulevard farces, who tries and fails to dupe a suggestible lass into falling in love with him. It was neither published nor produced. In 1789 Saint-Just did manage to publish an ambitious, mock epic, *Organt*, in two volumes of rhyming verse. He wrote most of it in prison. After completing his studies at the Collège Louis-le-Grand in Paris, he had returned to his home in Blérancourt near Laon, then stole the jewelry of his widowed mother and, back in Paris, sold it to support some riotous living. His mother obtained a *lettre de cachet* to get him interned in Picpus, a house of correction, from September 1786 to March 1787. Apparently chastised, he threw himself into the Revolution at the local level and gained such a reputation that he was elected to the Convention in September 1792, becoming its youngest and most extreme member. But an attempt to comb through *Organt* for previews of Saint-Just's revolutionary radicalism yields little—some mockery of religion, chivalry, the French court, and the Académie française, but no sustained political or social criticism. Its salient passages are pornographic. It reads as an attempt at a *succès de scandale* in the manner of Voltaire's *Pucelle*, but it has none of his wit, and the public paid no attention to it. As Saint-Just confessed in his preface, "I am twenty years old; I have botched this work; I will be able to do better."[26]

This quick tour of prerevolutionary careers among some of the most radical Jacobins indicates that they had literary ambitions and moved in and out of Grub Street, but, with the exception of Fabre, their writings did not express the hostility to the established order that I posited in 1971. To be sure, other writers who became Jacobins did indeed produce libels and seditious tracts before the Revolution. Pierre Louis Manuel, whose career is discussed at length in the following chapters, provides a typical example of the hacks in the literary underground who published and peddled works outside the law. Yet their careers reveal only the vertical dimension of the Republic of Letters. I think we should also consider horizontal relations—that is, the tension between the center and the margins.

The writer who best illustrates marginality is Simon-Nicolas-Henri Linguet, the most notorious journalist of the 1770s and 1780s.[27] After demonstrating precocious talent as a student and gaining experience abroad in various posts, Linguet tried to make his name as an author. He considered his *Histoire du siècle d'Alexandre* (1762) and *Théâtre espagnol* (1768) worthy of winning election to the Académie française. But the Academy rejected him; he quarreled with its secretary, d'Alembert; and he threw his lot in with the enemies of

the Enlightenment by accusing the philosophes of monopolizing positions of power and prestige.[28] At the same time, he
took up the law. In a serious of spectacular cases, beginning
with his defense of the chevalier de la Barre in 1766 (Linguet
won the admiration of the public, although he failed to save
la Barre from being executed for sacrilege), he demonstrated
a formidable talent as an orator—and outspoken contempt
for his colleagues. A particularly sharp attack on Pierre-
Jean-Baptiste Gerbier, France's most prominent lawyer, led
to Linguet's expulsion from the Paris bar in 1775.[29] He then
took up journalism, pouring scorn on his many enemies in
the *Journal de politique et de littérature*. He was forced to resign
from the *Journal* after again sniping at the Academy, and
emigrated to London and then Brussels, where he published
a journal of his own, *Annales politiques, civiles, et littéraires*, in
1777. Its verve and iconoclasm made it an enormous success.
Linguet kept it going until 1792, despite endless difficulties,
including two years of imprisonment in the Bastille after
he ventured into Paris in 1780. His *Mémoires sur la Bastille*
(1782), a powerful bestseller published from exile, where he
resumed the *Annales*, reinforced his appeal as a defiant critic
of the established order. He never sank into Grub Street. Far
from it, he gained wealth and fame; but he failed to win a
place at the center of power and prestige. He remained the
ultimate outsider.

Linguet's swashbuckling career made him the most
famous French writer, Pierre-Augustin Caron de Beaumarchais and Mirabeau included, during the last two decades
of the ancien régime. His *Annales*, reprinted and pirated
from many locations, won him an enormous readership and
earned him a fortune. He did not attack the Crown (Marie

Antoinette was rumored to enjoy his articles) or the ministers (he had defended the much-hated Chancellor Maupeou in 1774). Instead, he argued in favor of increasing the government's power and reducing aristocratic privileges in order to relieve the suffering of the peasant masses.[30] He concentrated his fire on corporate bodies—the *parlements*, the order of Parisian lawyers, and any institution that bore "the fatal name of Academy," in the sciences and fine arts as well as literature.[31] The academies incensed him most, because they had been taken over by the philosophes, whose power extended everywhere: "In France, there was nothing that was not subjected to it [the party of the philosophes]. The ministry, the law courts, science, literary circles, it had invaded everything. It dominated everything, even reputations. It alone opened the door to glory and wealth."[32]

This message had enormous appeal for other marginal writers. While struggling to get ahead in the world of letters, Brissot fell under Linguet's spell and defended him in an anonymous pamphlet, *Un Indépendant à l'ordre des avocats* (An independent to the order of lawyers), which opened with a defiant attack on privileged bodies in general: "I am nothing; I am connected with nothing; I ask for nothing. Therefore, I will tell the truth. The isolated man, the Independent, is the only one who has the power to tell it and the right to be believed."[33] Brissot sought out Linguet and attempted to collaborate with him (he got as far as writing an index to a volume of the *Annales*), but their paths diverged in the colony of French expatriates in London, where Brissot fell in with some buccaneering pamphleteers. Still, Brissot always admired Linguet's independent spirit. During the Revolution when he wrote his memoirs, he reminisced, "Ah! Linguet!

Linguet! . . . I loved to see you smash the proud despotism of exclusive bodies."[34]

The notion of the "Indépendent," the writer who defied privileged bodies and proclaimed unorthodox truths, fit the situation of many marginal writers, some trapped in poverty, others well off. Antoine-Joseph Gorsas typified the former. He scraped together a living as a schoolmaster in Versailles while turning out poems and pamphlets.[35] In burlesque tracts about the exhibitions of paintings in the biennial salon sponsored by the Royal Academy of Painting and Sculpture, he adopted the personage of Chrysostôme Critès, a cobbler-poet and "poor devil" from the ranks of the "hack composers of verse." Sometimes accompanied by an ass, Critès marched through the salons, holding forth about art with a provocative bravado that made the Academy and its domination of the art world look ridiculous.[36] In 1788 Gorsas joined the stable of hack writers who produced radical pamphlets under the name of Mirabeau, and he published *La Cour plénière*, a powerful attack on the ministry of Étienne-Charles de Loménie de Brienne. His seditious activities (and possibly some kind of scandal in the Versailles school) led to Gorsas's confinement in Bicêtre, a notoriously nasty prison. Soon after his release in 1789, he withdrew into a garret and, according to Lenoir, the former head of the Paris police, lived by writing libels and peddling forbidden books.[37] In July he launched one of the Revolution's most popular journals, *Le Courrier de Versailles à Paris et de Paris à Versailles* (later *Le Courrier de Paris dans les provinces et des provinces à Paris*). An early Jacobin, he eventually supported the Girondists and, after their overthrow, he was guillotined as one of their partisans on October 7, 1793.

Jean-Louis Carra, a friend of Gorsas and Brissot, was cut from the same cloth and followed a similar route into revolutionary journalism and Jacobinism.[38] Difficulties in his early life (imprisonment under an accusation, later dismissed, for a theft) led to a precarious existence as a proofreader and occasional writer in printing shops outside France and then as an adventurer in Eastern Europe. But by 1789 he had put Grub Street behind him, having gained a steady income and a respectable position in the Bibliothèque du Roi (King's Library). He published serious, ambitious works, notably *Le Système de la raison, ou le prophète philosophe* (The system of reason, or the philosopher-prophet) (1782), laying claim to be a philosophic luminary, although he never gained acceptance in the ranks of the philosophes. In *Nouveaux principes de physique* (New principles of physics) (1781–1783), he pretended to have outdone Newton as a physicist. But the Academy of Sciences refused to recognize his cosmological speculations, and his anger as an outsider shows through in the libels he published on the eve of the Revolution: *L'An 1787, ou précis de l'administration de la Bibliothèque du roi sous M. Lenoir* (The year 1787, or a short account of M. Lenoir's administration of the King's Library) (1787) and *M. de Calonne tout entier* (M. de Calonne in his entirety) (1788). His *Annales patriotiques et littéraires de la France* made him one of the most influential revolutionary journalists. Like Gorsas, he threw his lot in with the Girondists, and after their downfall, he was guillotined.

Jean-Paul Marat was a more extreme Jacobin and a more serious scientist than Carra. Far from sinking into indigence, he pursued a successful career as a doctor, first in England, then in France, where in 1777 he was named médecin des gardes du corps du comte d'Artois (doctor to the corps of guards to the comte d'Artois).[39] After years of experimentation, he sought recognition by the Academy of Sciences for discoveries about the nature of light, fire, and electricity. From 1778 to 1780, committees of the Academy investigated his work. In the end, it pronounced that it could not verify all his experiments and would not sanction his theories. He had expounded them in a handsome and legally published volume, *Découvertes de M. Marat . . . sur le feu, l'électricité et la lumière* (1779). In it, he, too, claimed to have superseded Newton, but he spoke respectfully of "this great man" and deferentially about the Academy. Having invented a new science, "la péroptrique" (with subdivisions such as "la catoptrique," "la dioptrique" and "l'opisoptrique"), he knew that his discoveries would upset those who held orthodox views, but he expected to prevail, thanks to the soundness of his experiments.

In a second edition published after his failure to win the Academy's backing, Marat appealed to the "supreme tribunal" of public opinion.[40] He maintained a moderate tone in his subsequent scientific works, such as *Notions élémentaires d'optique* (1784) and even a political tract, *Eloge de Montesquieu*, which he submitted, unsuccessfully, to an essay contest sponsored by the Academy of Bordeaux in 1785. But he expressed his bitterness at academicians, especially the philosophes who dominated the academies, in his private correspondence: "Since they neglect nothing to extend their unfortunate empire, they are increasing in number and in many forms. Our faculties, our academies are full of them, and without being able to avoid them, I have had to confront them in all of my enterprises."[41] His anger finally boiled over in *Les Charlatans modernes, ou lettres sur le charlatanisme académique*, published in 1791 but written before the Revolution. In it he vilified the leading members of the Academy of Sciences and also of the Académie française, because they were all frauds: they monopolized pensions and honors, while persecuting isolated geniuses, like Rousseau, who produced the only true advance in knowledge. All academicians were parasites, "making the rounds of social circles, acclaimed by the trumpets of fame, fattened up by the government, and devouring . . . the subsistence of the miserable artisan and the poor farmer."[42]

It would be possible to cite many other writers who lived on the margins of the world of letters yet did not inhabit Grub Street. Mathieu Pidansat de Mairobert serves as a last example, because he wrote and collaborated on several bestsellers in the underground book trade of the 1770s and 1780s: *Anecdotes sur Mme la comtesse du Barry* (1775), *Journal historique de la révolution opérée dans la constitution de la monarchie française par M. de Maupeou, chancelier de France* (1774–1776), *L'Observateur anglais, ou correspondance secrète entre Milord All'Eye et Milord All'Ear* (1777–1778), *Correspondance secrète et familière de M. de Maupeou avec M. de Sor**** (1771–1771), *Mémoires de M. l'abbé Terrai* (1777), and the 36-volume journal of gossip and public affairs, *Mémoires secrets pour servir à l'histoire de la République des lettres en France* (1777–1789).[43] Despite their scurrilous and gossipy character— or because of it—these libels spread a hostile view of the reign of Louis XV, particularly during the "revolution" of the judicial system by Chancellor Maupeou in 1771–1774. Although qualified to practice law, Mairobert supported himself from administrative positions (*commissaire de la* *marine* and later *secrétaire des commandements de M. le duc de Chartres*). He also served as a censor, although he was removed from his post for misconduct in 1761. According to a notice about his death by his successor as editor of the *Mémoires secrets*, he was protected by Malesherbes, the head of the book trade administration, and by several lieutenant generals of police.[44] As a favorite in the worldly salon of Mme Marie-Anne Doublet, where the *Mémoires secrets* originated, he cut something of a figure among the café regulars who tended to favor the Parlement of Paris in its quarrels with the government.

Despite these connections with a worldly and wealthy milieu, Mairobert was a *frondeur* (agitator) who lived on the edge of disaster. On July 2, 1749, he was arrested for distributing seditious verse about Mme de Pompadour, Louis xv, and the government. He spent nearly a year in the Bastille. His brother, who provided information to the police, said Mairobert refused to have any contact with his family or to follow a conventional career in the law. Before his arrest, Joseph d'Hémery, the police inspector in charge of the book trade, put Mairobert down as a suspicious character: "He said in the Café Procope while discussing the recent reform [the reorganization of the officer corps of the army], that any soldier who could do so should send the court to bugger off for good, because it only cares about devouring the common people and committing injustices. . . . This Mairobert is one of those who spreads the nastiest talk in Paris." Other reports indicated that Mairobert made a habit of collecting and distributing seditious verse. A police spy who had engaged him in conversation noted, "In a discussion about the risks taken by the author of such writing, he replied that he took none at all, that it was merely a matter of slipping something into the pocket of someone in a café or the theater or of dropping copies along public walks."[45] Mairobert also took risks in financial speculations. On March 27, 1779, after being compromised in a settlement after the notorious bankruptcy of the marquis of Brunoy, he went to a bathhouse, shut himself in a tub, sliced open a vein, and ended his life with a pistol shot.[46]

Although Mairobert disappeared before 1789, he contributed to the cacophony of messages that fed into the Revolution from the margins as well as the bottom of the literary world. Their common element was hostility to the cultural barriers that had kept outsiders outside. This passion provided much of the energy behind the revolutionary campaign against privilege, particularly in the realm of culture—privileges for books, journals, theaters, and academies.

The National Convention abolished the academies on August 8, 1793. In arguing for their suppression, Jacques-Louis David attacked the Academy of Painting and Sculpture and academies in general as the "the last refuge of all the aristocracies."[47] Abbé Grégoire, who drafted the report adopted by the Convention, condemned the Académie française for "the pretention of monopolizing glory, of keeping to itself the exclusive privilege of talent." He argued that it violated the basic principle of the Republic of Letters: openness and equality. Moreover, it victimized the writers who deserved most from the French republic: "Your hearts will certainly be moved," he said in a speech to the Convention, "in learning that several men of letters, worn out by long work and burning with patriotism, are struggling against destitution. National compensation should go only to those who are worthy of it; and after rejecting the vile courtiers of despotism, we must seek out merit in its basement dwelling or its sixth floor garret."[48]

Grégoire himself had not suffered in a garret, nor had other leading Jacobins, including Maximilien Robespierre. Many different paths led to Jacobinism. But the route through Grub Street appeared particularly important to the radicals of 1793, as Grégoire emphasized in his conclusion: "Almost always, true genius is sans-culotte."[49]

I would conclude my own argument on a similar note. The "Rousseau du ruisseau" did indeed inject passion into the ideological mix that drove Jacobinism. That energy was also generated by outsiders, who remained consigned to the margins of literary life, though they escaped Grub Street. Writers exerted a powerful force in undermining the ancien régime, not simply by advocating the ideas of the Enlightenment but also by expressing the contradictions inherent in the Republic of Letters.

HAVING REVISED the argument that launched me on the study of writers fifty-three years ago, I would like to introduce this volume with some brief remarks. Seen at a distance of three centuries, the rise of the writer appears as a crucial force in the making of the modern world. Writers represented a new kind of power: mastery over the media at a time when public opinion began to determine affairs of state and when literature touched the inner lives of an expanding readership. Yet writers had no well-defined place in the old regimes of Europe, as can be seen most clearly in the case of France. From the early seventeenth century, when France dominated international affairs, French literature set the style everywhere in Europe. By the end of the eighteenth century, most of the European elite read French books and followed the careers of French authors, not only Voltaire and Rousseau but also lesser figures like Linguet and Mercier. Famous as they were, those writers and hundreds of others did not fit easily into the institutional landscape of the ancien régime. They had no distinct social status, no common source of support, not even a shared sense of vocation, except among the philosophes and their emulators. Despite their lack of a collective identity, however, they filled the public sphere with their writings, their polemics, and their scramble to make a name for themselves. This book describes their lot—systematically, by showing the size and the shape of the literary population during the second half of the eighteenth century, and sociologically, by tracing patterns of careers. It does not pretend to rewrite literary history, but it follows careers through the great explosion of 1789 in a way that indicates how literature was revolutionized.

The eighteenth-century notion of a writer (*écrivain*) and author (*auteur*) was defined in the standard dictionary of the Académie française simply as someone who had written a book.[50] But contemporaries used a rich vocabulary to describe different varieties of authorship. *Homme de lettres* (*gens de lettres* in the plural, *femme de lettres* was rarely used) suggested participation in the refined world of letters. By announcing on its title page that it was written "par une société de gens de lettres," the *Encyclopédie* signaled its intellectual respectability. *Littérateur* indicated an identification with literature, understood as writing within elevated genres. In *De la littérature et des littérateurs*, Mercier emphasized the *littérateur*'s dedication to a calling, the moral improvement of humanity. Yet he also insisted on commitment to a career, using simpler terminology: "One exclaims everywhere that the number of authors is enormous. . . . But in fact there are not more than thirty writers in France who make [writing] a career."[51] The notion of a career, however, could be pejorative, particularly when it involved writing to make money. Voltaire, who was independently wealthy by 1750, pilloried his enemies as hacks who treated literature as a "métier" or "carrière" (job or career) and fought off starvation by attempting to live by their pens.[52] The French had many words for "scribbling" or "scrawling" hacks: "écrivailleur," "plumitif," "folliculaire," "gribouilleur," and (Voltaire's favorite) "pauvre diable." The language pointed to the existence of an underworld of scribblers located far beneath "le monde," where Voltaire believed literature should be located.

The broad range of the terminology indicates the problematic position of writers within the social order. Anyone who published anything could claim to be an author, but no one considered authors as professionals. They did not have to satisfy any entrance requirements, undergo an apprenticeship, receive certification, or belong to a corporate body. (Membership in an academy or a masonic lodge could not be compared with participation in a guild or the bar of lawyers.) Many pursued writing as an occupation, although for different reasons—to win honor, to achieve a certain standing (they often wrote *homme de lettres* after their names to indicate their *qualité* on official documents), or to make money. Many more combined writing with other employment, whether modest (work as a secretary or a corrector in a printing shop) or elevated (membership in a *parlement* or in the upper clergy). Some published books and then renounced writing after failing to make a success of it. Others published work off and on as occasions arose or for their private pleasure. Although contemporaries often referred to careers within the world of letters, there was no clearly demarcated route to success. Election to the Académie française represented the supreme achievement of many careers, yet the Académie included dignitaries like the count of Clermont, who never published anything and could barely spell.

Conditions changed throughout the century, as wealth, literacy, and the book market expanded. It would be inaccurate, however, to describe the change as a shift from a system based on patronage to one where writers lived by their pens. In the long run, the market may be said to have liberated writers from subservience to protectors, although varieties of protection still exist today, notably in universities, which provide a regular income to many authors of fiction. Before the Revolution, French writers commonly aspired to be assimilated in polite society, adopting the manners and the tone of "le monde" in conformity with the style set in the seventeenth century. The fusion of "gens de lettres" and "gens du monde" was a theme championed by Voltaire and played out in salons. Few authors asserted the "droits d'auteur," or proprietary rights to their writing, not even during the debates surrounding the reforms of the book trade in 1723 and 1777. Far from embracing the pursuit of profit, they generally subscribed to values like *honnêteté* and *politesse*, which had dominated salon life since the reign of Louis xiv.[53]

What distinguished the writers' understanding of their lot in the eighteenth century was a stronger sense of its dignity and of the glory to be won by a successful career. To be sure, Voltaire had celebrated Pierre Corneille, Jean Racine, and Molière as the architects of the grandeur of the "grand siècle," the century of Louis XIV.[54] But in doing so, he asserted the importance of their successors, whose commitment to literature was bound up with a higher cause, the spread of enlightenment. Voltaire's own celebrity as the supreme leader of the philosophes increased the appeal of literature as a vocation. One of the many tributes to his glory celebrated it for raising the dignity of *gens de lettres* in general:

> Vous [gens de lettres] qui nous éclairez, connaissez tous vos titres!
> D'un bout du monde à l'autre on entend votre voix,
> Vos accents vont frapper les oreilles des rois.[55]
> (You [men of letters] who enlighten us, know your rightful title!
> From one end of the earth to the other, one hears your voice,
> Your words have reached the ears of kings.)

Mercier expressed the same sense of mission in *De la littérature et des littérateurs*: "The influence of writers is such that they can now proclaim their power openly and no longer disguise the legitimate authority that they have over minds. Soundly established on the basis of the public interest and of the true understanding of man, they will direct the ideas of the nation."[56]

Notions of the power and prestige of writers became attached in the midcentury years to the figure of the philosophe. Although it had acquired many meanings since antiquity, the term became identified with an ideal type in *Le Philosophe*, an anonymous tract published in 1743.[57] In his modern form, the anonymous author argued, the philosophe was a freethinker, hostile to religion and all dogma, skeptical of received ideas, guided by his reason, and, as a social being, a member of polite society, unlike the *savant* who stayed in his study. The text was reprinted, after being trimmed to get past the censors, in the *Encyclopédie* and again in Voltaire's *Les Lois de Minos* (1773). It perfectly suited the Voltairean style of Enlightenment and a view that identified the modern man of letters with the philosophe.

The philosophes certainly attracted a great deal of attention during the midcentury decades. They became public figures, a favorite subject of gossip, pamphleteering, and even the stage (*Les Philosophes* was a hit at the Comédie française in 1760). Their notoriety thrived from scandals—particularly the polemics accompanying the publication and suppression of the *Encyclopédie* from 1751 to 1759. Bonfires of banned books inflamed public opinion, while persecution—enough to keep them in the public eye but not to silence them—made the philosophes into heroes for the generation of writers who came of age after the 1750s, when enlightened ideas were widely assimilated and the *Encyclopédie* sold openly.

In fact, the philosophes occupied so much space in public life that they crowded out many other writers, at least in the view of historians, who with good reason see the eighteenth century as the age of Enlightenment. But the great majority of writers did not join the ranks of the philosophes. They wrote the ordinary kinds of books that sold on the marketplace, and they formed the bulk of the population that needs to be surveyed in an account of authors in general. From this perspective, the success of the philosophes is important primarily as a factor that increased the attraction of writing as a career and the number of aspirants who adopted it.

To understand the writer's lot, it is best to begin with the examination of careers. They varied endlessly, of course, and the choice of cases to study is bound to be arbitrary—determined in large part by the availability of documentation. I have selected three examples that illustrate career patterns at different levels of success and failure. In each case study, the sources are rich enough to show how writers coped with concrete problems—how to get a first foothold, rise through the ranks, recover from falls, and maintain existence at an identifiable niche within the literary world.

To be sure, notions of rising and falling can make literary vocations appear as nothing more than a struggle for survival. I do not want to dismiss the importance of talent and the literary qualities that made for success and failure, but I am not attempting to write a history of literature. My purpose in focusing on careers is to understand the rules of the game and the way it was played according to the perceptions of the players. Once those themes are clear, it will be possible to stand back and view the literary population as a whole, including estimates of its size and growth during the second half of the eighteenth century. Research on this scale has never been executed, despite the profusion of biographical and bibliographical studies, yet it is worth pursuing, intrinsically as an element in social history, and politically as an aspect of the heavily charged atmosphere on the eve of the Revolution.

To see how that climate developed, I have studied contemporary controversies about writers and writing during the years that immediately preceded and followed the explosion of 1789. Although they attracted a great deal of attention at the time, the polemics have since been forgotten, because they were lost in the greater arguments about the fate of France. They involved only bit players, yet they summoned up the deeper opposition between Voltaire and Rousseau, and that conflict, though expressed in literary language, exposed the cultural issues at the heart of the political struggle.

The seemingly straightforward attempt to assess France's literary population therefore leads to the consideration of culture itself as the cement that held the ancien régime together and that failed to hold when things fell apart in 1789. The full extent of the literary element in the French Revolution lies beyond the boundaries of this book. Yet the story of writers and writing can be followed by tracing the careers of our three authors after July 14, 1789. The concrete details of their experience show how the literary world was transformed for those who lived at the heart of it.

These themes could be developed at great length, taking account of nuances, exceptions, and objections. Rather than working them over exhaustively, however, I have trimmed my text to a minimum. It is meant as an essay, not a treatise—that is, as an attempt to try out an argument, to interpret a familiar subject in an unfamiliar light. In the eighteenth century, France invented the intellectual—a public person who combines the life of the mind with a critical stance toward the surrounding society.[58] Voltaire was the founder of a line that extends to Victor Hugo, Émile Zola,

Jean-Paul Sartre, and Michel Foucault. Yet Voltaire also belonged to a species that had developed centuries earlier and that proliferated in great numbers during the last decades of the ancien régime. This social animal came to be known as a writer, a person who composed books—not necessarily a public figure but usually someone who produced works that, like him or her, had a brief existence and then disappeared into obscurity. While celebrating Voltaire and his progeny, history has taken little account of the general run of writers. This book takes the measure of that population and shows how it became imbedded in history during a period of dramatic change.

CAREERS

The Ancien Régime

I F, AS MERCIER asserted, only thirty writers in France could live by their pens, how did the others make a living? Although literature was not a profession, contemporaries recognized it as a social phenomenon with points of entry, patterns of success and failure, and sources of income founded on the cultural institutions of the ancien régime. The best way to understand how writers fit into the institutional landscape is to follow some exemplary careers. Although this approach does not do justice to the aesthetic and intellectual qualities of their writing, it reveals the conditions they had to cope with, whether they achieved success, struggled in the middle ranks, or floundered in failure.[1]

Le Roi Voltaire

Career patterns derived from conditions established in the seventeenth century, but they acquired a particular character during the eighteenth century, when Voltaire demonstrated how writing could lead to extraordinary influence and fame.[2] At age twenty-four, Voltaire conquered Paris with his tragedy, *Oedipe* (1718), which made him appear as a successor to Corneille and Racine. Thanks to connections, some from his school days at Louis-le-Grand, and to his wit, which scandalized and delighted fashionable society, he cut a figure in *le monde*. He established a base in the salons, while his satirical verse and essays captured the attention of the general public. Voltaire spent months in the Bastille, but persecution, just enough of it to make him famous without clipping his wings, added to the attraction of his publications, especially the provocative *Lettres philosophiques* (1733–1734) and the naughty *La Pucelle* (manuscript copies circulated from about 1730). More ambitious works—*La Henriade* (1723), *Le siècle de Louis XIV* (1751), *Essai sur les moeurs* (1756)—added to the solidity of his reputation. By 1750, he had won a seat in the Académie française and an official position as historiographer of the king. For the next twenty-eight years, he dominated the republic of letters as if he were its king.[3] But he did not depend on his pen to make a living. Protections among *les grands*, a gigantic (and rigged) speculation on the lottery, and commercial investments made him independently wealthy, and he was willing to use his fame and fortune to help younger writers, those with enough talent and commitment to *philosophie*, to follow in his wake.

Before discussing the three exemplary careers, it is important to take note of the way Voltaire became a factor in the play of power that shaped the Republic of Letters in the second half of the eighteenth century. The case of Jean-François Marmontel, related in Marmontel's memoirs, shows how Voltaire cleared a path for one of his most eminent disciples. To be sure, Marmontel made literary life under the ancien régime appear in a soft, golden light, because he wrote his memoirs after 1789, when he had become a bitter victim of the Revolution. Allowing for that bias and taking into account Marmontel's exceptional talent, his memoirs can be read as a map of the stops along the route to success for a writer. Other writers followed different routes, but Marmontel's career is worth considering for the light it sheds on the landscape faced by all of them.

Born in 1723 into the family of a poor tailor in Bort-les-Orgues, Corrèze, Marmontel began his ascent from a modest position in the social order. He did so well in his studies that he was promoted through the ranks that normally led to the priesthood. He was tonsured as an abbé and promised the protection of the archbishop of Bourges, which was likely to lead to a well-endowed benefice. While advancing within the church, Marmontel read widely, tutored, and wrote poetry. After one of his poems failed to win in a prize competition (the Jeux Floriaux of Toulouse), he sent it to Voltaire as if he were appealing to the supreme judge in affairs of belles lettres. Voltaire replied with such encouragement that their exchange of letters turned into an extensive correspondence, and in the end Voltaire became Marmontel's protector, while Marmontel decided to become a man of letters instead of a priest.

Marmontel came to Paris in 1745, expecting to get a position arranged for him by Voltaire with Philibert Orry, the controller general of finances. When he arrived, however, he was stupefied to learn that Orry had just fallen from office, leaving him without any means of support. But Voltaire promised to look after him and asked what he proposed to write. Marmontel had no idea, so Voltaire offered advice: write a play. Success in the theater was the best way to make a name, and once his reputation was established, all sorts of possibilities would open up. Marmontel retired to a garret, living off literary odd jobs and writing in bed in order to save on heating expenses. Voltaire provided subsidies and free tickets to the Comédie française, where Marmontel perfected his understanding of how plays succeeded. Finally, he composed a tragedy, *Denys le tyran*. It was a hit, and his career was launched.

The memoirs traced all the steps that led from that breakthrough to a position at the summit of the literary world. Feted as a promising young playwright, Marmontel was swept up in dinner parties and salons where he learned "le ton, les usages du monde," which Voltaire considered as a crucial ingredient of literature.[4] He received subsidies from the duke of Duras, lodging from a tax farmer, and a regular place in the salon of Mme Geoffrin. With Voltaire's blessing, he became an intimate in the circle of the philosophes and a contributor to the *Encyclopédie*. An ally of the philosophes who had connections in the court introduced him to Mme de Pompadour. Flattered by one of his poems, she landed him an administrative position ("secrétaire des Bâtiments," or building secretary) that paid well and required little work. Then she arranged for him to receive a pension attached to the income from the *Mercure*. That led to the editorship of the *Mercure*, where Marmontel prospered for nearly two years.

In December 1759, Marmontel suffered his first misfortune. He was sent to the Bastille under suspicion of having composed a satirical poem against the duke of Aumont. In fact, he had not written it but had recited it from memory in the salon of Mme Geoffrin. That was enough, however, to warrant his arrest, for poets could not mock grandees with impunity, and Marmontel also lost his position on the *Mercure*. Yet his imprisonment lasted only eleven days and won him considerable sympathy as a victim of arbitrary power. The government even compensated him for the loss of his editorship with a pension of 3,000 livres, which freed him to spend more time on his own writing. (The French livre, abbreviated henceforth as L., was worth roughly a day's labor for an unskilled worker.) Marmontel published two successful works, *Bélisaire* (1767) and *Les Incas* (1777), which were cleared by the censors, although (to Voltaire's delight) they contained enough anticlericalism to offend the theology faculty of the Sorbonne. Marmontel's *Contes moraux* (1755–1759), a series of sentimental tales, reached a broad audience and brought him additional income. But he dismissed the money he received from the sale of his works as incidental ("*du casuel*") and drew most of his income from pensions and sinecures, which continued to arrive as his reputation grew.[5] He was elected to the Académie française, named historiographer of France, and became permanent secretary to the Academy with lodging in the Louvre and a salary of 4,500 L. a year. By then he had accumulated 130,000 L. in savings and had started a family. He married the niece of his close friend André Morellet who came with a dowry (she was eighteen, he fifty-four); bought a country house surrounded by gardens and orchards; and commuted between the country and Paris in a carriage of his own. "From that point on, until the Revolution," Marmontel commented, "I can barely express how much pleasure and charm life and society had for us."[6]

Although bathed in nostalgia about the supposed sweet life (*douceur de vivre*) of the ancien régime, Marmontel's story showed that success in literature was open to talent and was built on protections, rather than income derived from the marketplace. It helped, of course, to have the right ideas. Inspired by Voltaire, young men often tried to get ahead by enlisting in the ranks of the philosophes, but even the philosophes' enemies understood the necessity of navigating through a world shaped by privilege and clientelism. Elie Catherine Fréron, Voltaire's bête noire, survived by clinging to the privilege of his journal, *Année littéraire* under the protection of the countess of La Marck, just as Marmontel profited from the privilege and pensions attached to the *Mercure*.

A Success Story: André Morellet

The career of André Morellet ran parallel to Marmontel's, and it can be followed in greater detail, because Morellet made it a master theme of his memoirs. To be sure, he, like Marmontel, wrote his memoirs in a bitter frame of mind after the Revolution had destroyed the world in which he had flourished. But one can allow for that bias and correct it by referring to his correspondence, where the same theme appears in a different light.[7]

Born in Lyon on March 7, 1727, Morellet was the first of fourteen children in a family of modest means. His father, a paper merchant, could not afford to give him an advanced education, but in secondary school, a Jesuit *collège*, he received encouragement from a teacher, shone in class, won prizes, and discovered that by studying hard he could get ahead in life. At age fourteen, instead of being apprenticed and disappearing into the petite bourgeoisie, he was sent to a seminary in Paris. A prosperous uncle, known in the family as *le docteur* "because he read the gazette," knew the seminary's superior, a fellow Lyonnais, and persuaded him to accept André at a cost of 300 L. for one year with the prospect of a scholarship if he excelled in his studies.[8] André did. As the Séminaire des Trente Trois was a good launching pad for a career in the church and the church was the main avenue of advancement for a penniless provincial, Morellet got his first glimpse of the rewards that might await a bright young man who could please his superiors: a benefice, not just the *portion congrue* (standard income) of a country curate, which at that time came to only 300 L. a year, but a deaconate or a priory dispensed through the prelate who held the *feuille des bénéfices*, a state office in control of ecclesiastical appointments.

It hardly seemed likely that Morellet's career would have such a happy ending when he completed his baccalaureate in theology, but his chances looked better when he was accepted to prepare his *licence* in the Maison et société de Sorbonne, an elite body within the University of Paris, where a few scholarship students mixed with young aristocrats who were destined for top positions in the church. Morellet's classmates included Anne Robert Jacques Turgot, who had not yet shifted to a secular career in the administration, and Étienne-Charles Loménie de Brienne, who would become archbishop of Sens and chief minister of the government in 1787–1788. As he explained in his memoirs, daily contact with such future eminences raised his hopes that they would smooth his way to a benefice.

Morellet spent most of his undergraduate years in the library, devouring books—not just theological treatises, but works by John Locke, Pierre Bayle, George-Louis Leclerc de Buffon, and even Voltaire, all available in the abundant collections of the Maison de Sorbonne. He also mastered enough theology to excel in the disputations in which students defended their theses in order to obtain degrees in theology. But what was to become of an obscure but brilliant graduate of the Sorbonne in 1752? In fact, Morellet made it as far as the *licence* only by a stroke of luck. A cousin unexpectedly came into an inheritance from a retired ship captain and loaned Morellet 1,000 L. By taking a cheap garret room furnished with a few straw chairs and by refusing to follow his classmates to the opera and the theater, he made the sum stretch over five years. Meanwhile, his ideas changed. Having read his way through most of the works of the early Enlightenment, he found it impossible to become a parish priest, yet he also confronted the impossibility of living as a writer: "I did not consider myself to be in a position to live from the métier of a man of letters."[9] That left only one alternative: Morellet would remain in the church as an abbé but not a full-fledged priest, and he would take whatever intellectual employment the church could provide.

First, he knocked on the door of the Jesuits. The Père de la Tour, principal of the Collège Louis-le-Grand, received him "with all the haughtiness and dignity of a protector," and then turned him down for a tutoring job in Portugal, no doubt, Morellet later reflected, because as a young abbé he sounded too much like a future *philosophe*.[10] After a few more months of unemployment, he began to worry seriously about his daily bread. Then the abbé of Sarcey, his mentor in the Séminaire des Trente-Trois, came to his rescue by arranging for him to be the tutor of the younger son of the marquis of La Galaizière, chancellor of Lorraine and Barrois. The young man was taking the first steps that would eventually lead to the bishopric of Saint-Dié. He needed a veteran of the Sorbonne to guide him through his studies for the baccalaureate and *licence*. Thanks to de Sarcey's recommendation, Morellet was chosen for the job: 1,000 L. a year, with food and lodging in the Collège du Plessis.

From that time on, Morellet never again felt the pinch of poverty. By cultivating the right contacts, turning his contacts into protections, and transforming protections into pensions, he made himself a rich man. But it was a long, tortuous process, and he chronicled every stage of it in his memoirs.

Morellet took care to establish good relations with his pupil, who made it through each phase of a future bishop's education without a slip. The boy's father, satisfied with his progress, rewarded Morellet with a pension of 1,000 L. attached to the Abbey of Tholey. Morellet attempted to build on it by providing all sorts of "little literary services" to influential clergymen connected with the Collège du Plessis, but they led to nothing, because, as he later discovered, he had acquired an unfortunate reputation in ecclesiastical circles as an Encyclopedist.[11] He had befriended a like-minded young abbé, Jean Martin de Prades, who was writing articles on religious subjects for the *Encyclopédie*; de Prades introduced him to Diderot; and soon Morellet was keeping dubious company. Unfortunately, de Prades's article, "Certitude," in volume 2 seemed to be riddled with heresies, and the doctoral thesis that he defended in the Sorbonne in 1751 looked like flagrant encyclopedism to both the Jesuits and their enemies, the Jansenists (proponents of an austere, Augustinian strain of Catholicism), who outdid one another in condemning it and running de Prades out of the kingdom. Not only was Morellet willing to step into the gap left by de Prades, but he proved himself qualified for the job by publishing his first tract, *Petit écrit sur une matière intéressante* (1756), a Swiftian salvo against the persecution of Protestants in the Midi. "Delighted to see a priest mock intolerance," Diderot and Jean Le Rond d'Alembert set Morellet to writing articles on theological subjects, which he treated historically, in order to relativize dogma instead of expounding it as absolute truth.[12]

From May 1758 until March 1759, Morellet accompanied his pupil, La Galaizière, on a tour of Italy, paid for by the young man's father. While browsing in a theological library in Rome, he came upon the *Directorium inquitorum* by Nicolas Eymeric, a grand inquisitor of the fifteenth century. By excerpting its most hair-raising passages about torturing and burning heretics and by reordering them in a highly readable form, but without any commentary of his own, Morellet produced a *Manuel des Inquisiteurs* in which the Inquisition seemed to condemn itself. He sent a copy to Voltaire via d'Alembert and in return received the patriarch's blessing. "My dear brother," Voltaire wrote to d'Alembert in his mock-ecclesiastical style, "embrace for me the worthy brother who has produced this excellent work."[13] Morellet had been accepted into the brotherhood, the inner circle of philosophers who ran the Voltairian "church."

It was a prestigious position but an awkward one for a clergyman in the Church of Rome. When he returned to Paris in the spring of 1759, the *Encyclopédie*, condemned by the pope, the Parlement of Paris, and the king's council, had been officially declared dead, though it was secretly protected by the director of the book trade, Lamoignon de Malesherbes, while Diderot continued to work on the last ten volumes. Most of its contributors, including d'Alembert and Voltaire, jumped ship. Morellet did, too. He had no other choice, if he wanted to escape the fate of the abbé of Prades. Yet Morellet rallied to the cause of the philosophes in 1760 after they were attacked by two of their most vocal enemies—Jean-Jacques Lefranc de Pompignan, who denounced them for irreligion in the Académie française; and Charles Palissot, who ridiculed them in *Les Philosophes*, a play performed at the Comédie française. Morellet wrote three pamphlets against Pompignan and then raked over Palissot's private life in a pamphlet, *Préface de la comédie des Philosophes, ou la vision de Charles Palissot*. This libel landed him in the Bastille on June 11, 1760.

It gave offense not simply because it attacked Palissot, who was merely a writer and not worthy of being avenged by the state, but because it ridiculed someone of importance, Palissot's protector, the princess of Robecq. Although gravely ill, she had attended a performance of *Les Philosophes*; and Morellet mocked her as a religious bigot who had left her sick bed in order to see religion vindicated and the philosophes humiliated on the stage. Unfortunately, the princess died soon afterward, and Morellet was seen as having violated the standards of polite society by offending a great lady. As soon as he was locked up, he realized that he had jeopardized his entire career. His despair shows through a letter that he wrote from the Bastille to the head of the Parisian police: "By an act of folly, I have lost in twenty-four hours the consideration of my position and all the hopes for fortune that I could attain by it."[14] In his memoirs, however, he gave a very different account of his imprisonment:

> I saw the walls of my prison lit up by the possibility of some literary glory: persecuted, I would be better known. The men of letters whom I had avenged, and the philosophy for which I was a martyr, would begin to establish my reputation. Men of the world, who love satire, would give me a better reception than ever. A career would open before me, and I could follow it with a greater advantage. These six months in the Bastille would provide me with an excellent recommendation and would infallibly make my fortune.[15]

When seen from inside in 1760, the Bastille appeared very different from the royal residence—complete with a decent wine cellar, a good kitchen, and an excellent library—that Morellet conjured up in his imagination thirty-five years later, when he looked back at the ancien régime with the disasters of the Revolution fresh in his mind.

When Voltaire learned of Morellet's imprisonment, he pulled strings to get him released, noting, "It's a pity that such a good officer has been taken prisoner at the beginning of the campaign."[16] Other allies of the philosophes intervened, and after six weeks Morellet left the Bastille, not only as a free man but as something of a celebrity—the "abbé

Mords-les" (Father Bite-them) celebrated by Voltaire and a candidate for admission to the most fashionable salons in the city. He had already gained entry a few months earlier to the salon of Mme Geoffrin, thanks to an introduction by the powerful treasury official (intendant des finances), Trudaine de Montigny, to whom in turn he had been introduced by Turgot. Trudaine also helped him join the beaux esprits at the dinner table of Alexis Claude Clairault and the beau monde gathered around the clavichord of Mlle de Riaucourt. Turgot introduced him to the marquis of Chastellux, who introduced him to Buffon, and they all crossed paths again at the dinners of Mme Geoffrin. Turgot also helped Morellet take his first steps into the philosophic salons of d'Holbach and Helvétius and—with additional backing from their classmate, Boisgelin de Cicé, now archbishop of Aix—into the worldly salon of the countess of Boufflers: "Such introducers, and belles-lettres, which she loved, doubtlessly made her indulgent for my lack of familiarity with the manners of high society (le monde)."[17]

To frequent *le monde*, one had to master a certain variety of *politesse*. Morellet's memoirs show how he learned to play the game, picking up cues from his more worldly schoolmates, improvising *vers de circonstance* for the amusement of Clairault, complimenting the musicality of Mlle Riaucourt, listening respectfully to the countess of Boufflers read from her compositions, exchanging irreverent witticisms with the free spirits at d'Holbach's table, and repressing them within earshot of Mme Geoffrin. Success in the salons required a delicate balance of deference and wit and a good ear for the *ton du monde*. Morellet was a quick learner and struck just the right note.

After five years on the salon circuit, Morellet acquired such expertise that Mme Necker consulted him and two other veterans cut from the same cloth, Marmontel and the abbé Guillaume François Raynal, when she decided to mount a salon of her own. They helped her select an appropriate mixture of *gens de lettres* and *gens du monde*, and they also set the tone: good conversation of a belletristic kind and no loose talk about religion. By this time, Morellet's calendar was full:

Mondays: Mme Geoffrin (beaux arts)
Tuesdays: Mme Helvétius
Wednesdays: Mme Geoffrin (literature)
Thursdays: Maynon d'Invault and d'Holbach
Fridays: Mme Necker
Sundays: d'Holbach

In addition to these fixed engagements, Morellet also made frequent appearances in the salons of Mme de Boufflers, Mlle de Riaucourt, Mlle de Lespinasse, and Mme Suard. Many of these gatherings included dinner (from 2:00 to 4:00), and some were "soirees" (from 11:00 p.m. to 3:00 a.m.). Morellet could spend most of his waking hours at the tables and in the armchairs of the *gens du monde*, exchanging bright remarks about Italian versus German opera, the virtues of the *drame bourgeois*, and the latest squabbles between Voltaire and Rousseau. But where was it all leading?

On a visit arranged by Morellet, the young Milanese aristocrat Alessandro Verri came to Paris in 1766 with Cesare Beccaria, the celebrated author of the enlightened treatise *Of Crimes and Punishments*. Verri saw the salon performances with the eyes of an outsider. After accompanying Morellet, who served as translator to Beccaria, to Mme de Boufflers's, he wrote to his brother, "Our Morellet and Marmontel behave before her with a great deal of modesty. She is a lady who can determine who gets pensions. But this courtly atmosphere disgusted me."[18] For impecunious writers, salon life was above all a matter of fortune hunting. Morellet's fortune in the early 1760s came to 1,000 L. a year, the pension granted to him for overseeing the education of La Galazière. The pension covered all his needs—a laborer usually made from 300 to 500 L. a year—but it was not permanent and, in fact, it ceased to be paid in 1770.

In order to attain financial security, Morellet needed a protector. Thanks to the introduction from Turgot, Morellet developed a strong connection with the rich and powerful Trudaine family at the beginning of his career. The family's patriarch, Daniel Charles Trudaine, who died in 1769, and his son, Jean Charles Philibert Trudaine de Montigny, who died in 1777, dispensed lucrative sinecures and pensions attached to the trade bureau (bureau de commerce), a powerful state body that oversaw trade, where they held sway as royal officials (intendants de finance). They championed free trade and therefore opposed the state-sponsored monopoly of the East India Company and restrictions on the marketing of grain. Montigny also cut quite a figure in the salons, while his father, a more serious spirit, encouraged bright students with ministerial ambitions like Turgot and Loménie de Brienne to study political economy. Morellet followed suit because, as he explained in his memoirs, "Attached as I was to men whose ideas concerned useful objects, my own [ideas] naturally followed the same course."[19]

As he further explained in describing Trudaine de Montigny, "I owe to him the small fortune that made it possible for me to pass most of my life agreeably."[20] Political economy became the primary subject of his writings, the Trudaines the main object of his hopes for financial support. As soon as he got out of the Bastille, he made sure he had not damaged his relations with Trudaine père. He was reassured to learn that "I will still be just as good for employment at his various projects."[21] From then on, Morellet pursued the Trudaine line in a series of books, pamphlets, reports, and memoirs. When the Trudaines and their allies were in power, Morellet promoted government policy—notably under the ministries of Maynon d'Invault, Trudaine de Montigny's brother-in-law (1768–1769); Turgot (1774–1776); and Brienne (1787–1788). When their enemies gained control of the finance ministry—notably under Joseph-Marie Terray (1769–1774) and Jacques Necker (1779–1781)—he either sniped at the ministry from a safe distance or held his fire.

Writing government propaganda was less noble than battling for Enlightenment, at least in the eyes of some of Morellet's contemporaries. To Diderot, it made him look like a hired gun. "He has shown himself to be a vile mercenary who sells his pen to the government against [the interest of] his fellow citizens."[22] To the officials on the receiving end of his intra-ministerial memoirs, it sometimes made him look like a hack. After Morellet submitted one of his tracts to Trudaine de Montigny, who passed it on to the intendant of finances Chauvelin, who in turn gave it to the controller general Laverdy in 1764, Laverdy replied, "It's not up to an obscure writer, who often doesn't possess a hundred *écus* (coins worth 3 L. or the equivalent of three days wages for an unskilled laborer), to give lessons to men in power."[23] But it would be unfair to reduce Morellet's writings to self-interest. Everything suggests that he believed in the principles that he defended in his tracts. He had imbibed economic liberalism while sitting at the feet of Vincent de Gournay, the man who supposedly coined the phrase "laissez faire, laissez passer," and he devoted twenty years to the preparation of a five-volume *Dictionnaire de commerce*, which he intended to be the supreme work of his career. Although Morellet never completed this treatise, he expounded its ideas in many publications arguing for free trade and the destruction of monopolies. He was a talented free-trade advocate at a time when Physiocratic writing made economics an important question of public debate. There is no reason to doubt his dedication to the cause he advocated.

The fact that Morellet's economic writings coincided closely with the policies of his protectors may pose more of a problem for the modern reader than it was for Morellet. If his memoirs are to be believed, he never perceived any conflict between self-interest and ideological commitment. He proceeded from assumptions about writers and writing that antedated the romantic cult of genius. To him it was natural that a man of letters would scramble for protectors and scribble in their service. Instead of disguising the connection between publication and protection, he celebrated it. It was the key to his success, and as he was telling a success story in his memoirs, he developed the theme in glorious detail, free from any modern illusions about the sacred character of literature as a vocation.[24]

To trace this theme with all its variations would require a full-scale biography, but a few instances should show how it served to organize Morellet's narrative of his rise to riches. By 1768, when d'Invault became controller general, Morellet had demonstrated his ability to turn out politico-economic tracts on order. In 1758 he had produced some *Réflexions sur les avantages de la libre fabrication et de l'usage des toiles peintes* [Reflections on the advantages of the free production and use of painted canvas] and in 1762 a *Mémoire des fabricants de Lorraine et de Bar* [Memoir of the manufacturers of Lorraine and Bar] both for Trudaine père. D'Invault's ministry, supported by the duke of Choiseul, a friend of the philosophes, seemed to offer the Trudaine-Turgot clan a golden opportunity to clear away obstacles to freedom of trade. At d'Invault's instigation and with documentation supplied by the government bureaucracy, Morellet wrote a pamphlet demanding the suppression of the monopoly of the East India Company. Necker published a reply in defense of the company, and Morellet rebutted the reply so effectively in a second pamphlet that, he claimed, the government revoked the monopoly and the Parlement of Paris abandoned a plan to oppose the revocation. In fact, d'Invault probably had determined to destroy the East India Company in any case and merely used Morellet to prepare the way by winning over public opinion. But the opinion of the "public"—an ill-defined mixture of various social groups—had become crucial for the success of fiscal policies by the 1760s. No one appreciated its importance better than Necker, who had a personal stake in the East India Company and opposed free trade measures. To challenge Necker in a public polemic was to expose the salons to a great deal of conflict. Nevertheless, Necker did not take offense, and Morellet continued to frequent the Necker salon until 1779, when the Necker-Turgot rivalry made double allegiance impossible, and he withdrew. In the long run, this fidelity to the Trudaine-d'Invault-Turgot line proved profitable, but Morellet had to wait several years before collecting his reward. "This work did not win for me any recompense from the government, as the minister had been dismissed before having fulfilled his promises," he explained in the memoirs. "But five years later, with the arrival of M. Turgot in the ministry, I was given by an edict of the Council a perpetual payment of 2,000 L. on the trade bureau treasury (Caisse du commerce) 'for the publication of different works and memoirs about administrative matters.'"[25]

In fact, Morellet expected to get a great deal more from the d'Invault ministry: a permanent position with an income of 6,000 L. as secretary of the trade bureau (bureau de commerce). This office would bring not only financial security but also help in the preparation of his masterwork, the *Dictionnaire de commerce*, because he could use his position to gather commercial data from correspondents located everywhere in the French administration. Morellet lined up all his protectors: Trudaine père, who "was all-powerful in the administration of commerce"; Trudaine de Montigny, Morellet's constant companion in the salons; Michel Bouvard de Fourqueux, a powerful state councillor, whose two daughters had married d'Invault and Trudaine de Montigny; and d'Invault himself, who included Morellet in a Thursday salon devoted to political economy.[26] When the position became vacant in December 1768, Morellet cashed in all his chips: "I reminded M. Trudaine of his promises, M. de Fourqueux and M. d'Invault of their professed interest in me, to all of them the need I had of a position for my work."[27] But the job went to another protégé of d'Invault, Louis Paul Abeille, a manufacturing inspector.

This was a bitter blow to Morellet's career. He blamed it for his ultimate failure to complete his *Dictionnaire de commerce*, which he had announced in a gigantic prospectus published in May 1769. He continued to plug away at the *Dictionnaire* nonetheless, and he received plenty of help from the government, because he persuaded Trudaine de Montigny to compensate him with an annuity of 4,000 L. on the trade bureau treasury (Caisse du commerce)—a huge sum, which covered Morellet's living expenses as well as a secretary and a research assistant. This "indemnity," however, came with strings attached: "The minister of finance, who paid me, naturally could dispose of my time when he needed to. M. Trudaine de Montigny had the same right in his capacity as intendant of finance and commerce, and especially as my benefactor and my friend."[28]

The result was a series of polemical works, which Morellet wrote for a succession of ministers: *Réfutation de l'ouvrage qui a pour titre, Dialogue sur le commerce des bleds*, an attack on abbé Galiani written for Trudaine de Montigny and the duke of Choiseul; *Théorie du paradoxe* and *Réponse sérieuse à M. L[inguet]*, attacks on Simon Nicolas Henri Linguet written for Trudaine de Montigny and Turgot; and *Analyse de l'ouvrage intitulé De la législation et du commerce des grains*, an attack on Necker written for Turgot. The abbé "Mords-les" was ready to bite anyone who threatened the hands that fed him.

Not that he can be considered a hired propagandist. Far from it, he believed in the principles he defended, and his patrons needed defenders, because their measures stirred up controversy and exposed them to hostile gusts of public opinion. The *Théorie du paradoxe* showed Morellet at the top of his form, heaping scorn on Linguet, a formidable polemicist who opposed free trade in grain. By artfully arranging quotations from Linguet's publications, Morellet made him out to be "the grand master" of contradictions, inconsistencies, and absurdities, including the claim that the common people fared better under Asiatic despots than under French kings.[29] In addition to this dog fighting, Morellet also wrote all sorts of internal reports and memoranda for the Paris police and officials in the finance ministry, especially during the ministries of Turgot and Brienne, when he functioned as an advisor and intermediary between the government and various interest groups.

As the publications accumulated, the pensions followed. By 1776 Morellet had become a rich man, and he could assess his situation with a good deal of pride:

> I had succeeded in placing my brother in the Domaines administration, giving him, with some interests in financial affairs, eleven to twelve thousand livres in *rentes* (annuities). My annuity on the trade bureau treasury came to quite a lot; and including two thousand francs as compensation for my memoirs on the East India Company, I had six thousand livres plus a hundred pistoles [1,000 L.] from an annuity on the Abbey of Tholey that I received from the king of Poland by way of compensation for the debt of La Galaizière; and finally from time to time I got something for my little literary works.[30]

This passage, like many others in the memoirs, is revealing, not because it exposes the self-interest behind Morellet's writing but because it expresses an assumption located at the opposite extreme of the romantic cult of the writer—namely, that self-interest and writing should be allied. It also reveals a second assumption: that writers could not expect to make much money from the sale of their works. Although Morellet's "little literary works" included translations from English and Italian books and some belletristic essays, most of his writing was devoted to questions of political economy; and all of it was marketable. His translation of Beccaria's *On Crimes and Punishments* went through seven editions within a year, and his Paris publishers, the Estienne brothers, paid him 1,000 L. a year for his work on the *Dictionnaire de commerce* with the prospect of 15,000 L. when it was completed. Those were better terms than what Diderot received for the *Encyclopédie*. Yet nowhere in his memoirs or correspondence did Morellet mention the possibility of supporting himself from the sale of his works. He commented on a few incidents, such as the incompetence of his publishers in marketing his translation of Jefferson's *Notes on Virginia* and the happy experience of receiving a set of silver worth 6,000 L. from a group of merchants who had commissioned him to write a memoir against the restored East India Company in 1787.[31] But he always proceeded from the assumption that success in "the career of letters" came from pensions and sinecures.[32]

Success was a family affair. As the oldest of fourteen children, all as impecunious as himself, Morellet had plenty of family to look after. In 1777 he moved into a spacious townhouse, la maison neuve des Feuillants, rue Saint-Honoré (today numbers 219–235): twenty rooms, including three for the servants on the fifth floor, and a stable big enough for four horses. He invited his brother, Jean François, whom he had helped place in the lucrative office of cashier for the administration of the domains of the king; his widowed sister, Françoise, along with her daughter, Marie Adélaïde; and, a few years later, two other nieces. When Marie Adélaïde caught the eye of Morellet's friend Marmontel, Morellet and his brother put together a dowry of 20,000 L., and the newlyweds also moved in. Thus Morellet presided over an entire household, and on Sundays he invited a select company of writers, musicians, and artists to his dining table. After an abundant meal, they retired to a reception room overlooking the Tuileries Gardens. They listened to readings of *pièces de circonstance*, played music, and conversed. Morellet had created a salon of his own. He had arrived.

And more was to come. In 1777 Mme Geoffrin, the first lady of the salons, died, leaving Morellet a *rente viagère* (lifetime annuity) of 1,257 L. Morellet's circle of patrons even extended to England, where he had acquired the favor of Lord Shelburne during a visit financed by Trudaine de Montigny in 1772. Morellet became Shelburne's Paris correspondent, supplying him with regular reports on life in the capital. In 1782, Shelburne assumed power as prime minister in Britain. After negotiating the Treaty of Versailles to end the American war, he asked the count of Vergennes, France's foreign minister, to arrange for Morellet to receive an abbey—a reward, Shelburne explained, for "liberalizing" his ideas on foreign trade. Morellet had been trying for years to get an abbey—that is, the income from a benefice as an *abbé commendataire* (nonresident abbot), one of the most notorious abuses of the church under the ancien régime—but his reputation as an Encyclopedist kept getting in his way when his name came up before the unenlightened prelates who held the *feuille des bénéfices* through which such largesse was dispensed. Vergennes decided to avoid the complexities of ecclesiastical lobbying and simply issued another pension to Morellet: 4,000 L. more a year, drawn from the finance ministry.

This pension had the additional advantage of leaving the way clear for an eventual benefice. Charles Antoine de La Roche-Aymon, the reactionary archbishop of Reims who had administered the *feuille des bénéfices*, died in 1777. His successor, Yves Alexandre de Marbeuf, bishop of Autun, was not allergic to Encyclopedists and had known Morellet as a student in the Collège du Plessis, but Morellet had to wait for his card to come up in the general reshuffling that took place in the *feuille des bénéfices*. The card was an *induit*, or claim to the succession of a benefice, which Turgot had granted to Morellet in 1769. After a great deal of bartering and trading, the *induit* was settled on the priory of Thimert near Chartres, one of the richest in Marbeuf's juridiction. To Morellet's delight, the current prior was "old and sickly," and he soon died. Morellet came into a lordly estate with 16,000 L. in revenue and "all the seigneurial rights of the hunt, *cens* [an annual payment levied on peasants], and honorific *rentes*." [33] He had become a seigneur, living off what the Revolution was soon to abolish as "feudalism," and he meant to enjoy it.

The memoirs recount in loving detail Morellet's remodeling of his dream house in the country.

> At my age [then 62], it was natural to be in a hurry to enjoy things. As soon as I had taken possession [of the priory], I returned to Paris to arrange everything that would embellish my new establishment. Back in Thimert in mid-July [1788], I bought the furnishings of my predecessor for two

thousand livres, and I brought in masons, joiners, and carpenters; I employed a wallpaper hanger from Réveillon [a notable manufacturer of fine wallpaper], who worked for six weeks; I hired an upholsterer from Dreux, who completed the furnishing except for some pieces that I brought from Paris. I also began laying out my garden with new plantings and water works. As the area had no springs, I set up large basins to collect rainwater; the water from the well was also excellent. I had everything repaired; nothing was forgotten. At last, after having spent about two months to embellish and complete my little hermitage, using all the energy that God has given me—and it's not nothing—I was in a state to enjoy two happy months until All Saints Day.[34]

One year before the fall of the Bastille, Morellet had come to enjoy the ancien régime in all its famous "*douceur de vivre*" (sweetness of living). He calculated his annual income at "nearly thirty thousand livres in *rentes*, in benefices, and in pensions." It can be broken down roughly as follows, using Morellet's calculations:

2,000 L. Annuity on the trade bureau treasury arranged by Turgot

4,000 L. Indemnity on the trade bureau treasury given by Trudaine de Montigny

1,000 L. Payments by the Estiennes for the preparation of the *Dictionnaire de commerce*

1,275 L. *Rente* given by Mme Geoffrin

4,000 L. Pension arranged by Shelburne and Vergennes

16,000 L. Income from the priory of Thimert

28,275 L.[35]

Morellet certainly had accumulated a fortune, but the way he pieced it together was not as painless as he made it seem in his memoirs. Writing after the Revolution, which destroyed nearly everything he had amassed, he described the ancien régime as a paradise, where pensions dropped like plums. Thus, his account of receiving the priory of Thimert: "That fortune, which I can say I never sought although I hoped to receive it, came to me out of nowhere and with greater benefit than I could have expected or imagined."[36] In fact, Morellet had begged, cajoled, maneuvered, and intrigued for a benefice throughout the previous thirty years. Every step of his career, every pension in his account books cost him endless lobbying in the antechambers of *les grands*.

To follow that process, one must put Morellet's memoirs aside and study his correspondence. There he strikes a different range of tones, sometimes bitter, often urgent, nearly always worried, and on some occasions desperate. Literature is a "battle field,"[37] the chase for pensions one "unhappiness" after another, the struggle for protections an endless source of disappointment.[38] In writing to Lord Shelburne, Morellet laments about the "powerful friends that I have in my fatherland and who have neglected me in such a shameful way."[39] In writing to Turgot, he complains bitterly about Trudaine de Montigny's failure to extract a sinecure for him by lobbying with d'Invault: "Imagine how sad it is for me at the age of forty-two to think that I can arrive at an old age without a roof over my head. It is necessary for my friends, those who truly are friends, to do something to procure a benefice for me. . . . Think of that yourself."[40]

The themes of disappointment, danger, the fragility of his situation, the threat of destitution in his old age recur again and again. Unlike the Morellet of the memoirs, the Morellet of the correspondence does not know how his story will turn out. As he presents his situation in the letters, every step can bring disaster, every success can be reversed. He worries about overplaying his hand in the polemics with Necker and underrating Galiani's ability to make *laissez-faire* look laughable. At one point he is ready to risk all on Rohan patronage in Alsace, at another on Champion de Cicé's hold on benefices in Rodez. He constantly pins his hopes on the Trudaine family and always fears that they will let him down. His writings identify him with their free-trade policies, but he worries that he has overcommitted himself to that line. Shouldn't he prepare an escape route by cultivating their enemy, abbé Terray? Shouldn't he warm up more to Turgot's rival, Necker? False steps, wrong turns, misplaced allegiances threatened Morellet's career at every point, because his fortune was tied to the favor of *gens en place* (men in power).

Both Mme Geoffrin and Malesherbes had warned him that his pensions could collapse like a house of cards if a minister fell out of favor. So, when Terray replaced d'Invault in the finance ministry in 1769, Morellet was seized with panic. Terray stood for the opposite of the free trade policies favored by d'Invault. No matter: Morellet could adapt himself to the new ministry. He merely needed to have his way prepared by some carefully placed compliments; he wanted an introduction to Terray, a private audience, an opportunity to make his case and fend off the "the dangers that menace me."[41] The fall of Choiseul in 1770 precipitated the same reaction. Morellet expected to be stripped of all his pensions and exposed to a "a poor and painful old age."[42] He suddenly saw himself naked, "as poor as Job at the age of forty seven."[43] His only hope was for a benefice, which might be snared by winning over the chancellor Maupeou (who stood for the opposite of Choiseul's policies) and Champion de Cicé, his classmate who had become archbishop of Rodez: "He spoke to me about an abbey in Aurillac belonging to the bishop of Troyes, who, it's said, is very sickly, and on which an *induit* could easily be placed."[44]

When Turgot took over the state finances in 1774, Morellet thought that at last his time had come and immediately bombarded the new minister with requests for favors. His first thought was for Abeille's job in the financial bureaucracy, which he had continued to covet ever since his defeat in the lobbying for it five years earlier. But he would settle for various pensions and benefices—a new subsidy in the trade bureau, any one in a series of abbeys that he carefully listed in a memorandum, a stipend attached to the *Mercure*, a position for his brother that would pay for the dowry of their niece, almost any kind of "durable and solid property that would shelter me from misfortune—what is known as baked bread."[45] Morellet had known Turgot long enough and well enough to plead with remarkable frankness. "I am thinking of the future, . . . of old age that is approaching, of my family, which I do not want to leave unhappy. In short, I no longer have a calm spirit, free from worry about money."[46] The anxious, hungry pamphleteer of the correspondence looks very different from the rich uncle and salon lion of the memoirs.

But neither the memoirs nor the correspondence provides a pure, unmediated picture of Morellet's carer. They need to be read against each other, as different kinds of texts, each with a rhetorical slant of its own. For all their immediacy, Morellet's letters are carefully constructed documents. Their style shows how Morellet adapted his language to the circumstances in which he wrote. He was frank to Turgot, courtly to Vergennes, smarmy to Shelburne, bantering to Franklin, and Voltairean to Voltaire. The consistently mellow tone of the memoirs suited a narrative designed to bring out the Augustan qualities of literary life under the ancien régime. Its fictitious character is obvious, if one compares it with the correspondence. Yet the fiction was not false: it merely expressed the distortions built into a view that looked back at the reigns of Louis XV and Louis XVI across the trauma of the Revolution.

With that corrective in mind, one can assess Morellet's account of the last stage of his career before 1789. In 1785 he reached the apogee of success by winning election to the Académie française. True, he had not completed his *Dictionnaire de commerce*, and his writings consisted mostly of polemical works on political economy, Voltairean pamphlets, and translations. But he had written more than many members of the Academy, and in any case a seat had been reserved for him by the academicians who rubbed elbows with him in the salons: Marmontel, Jean-Baptiste-Antoine Suard, Jean François de La Harpe, Jacques Delille, Bernard-Joseph Saurin, and François-Jean de Chastellux.

Morellet also became a kind of éminence *grise* to his old schoolmate, Loménie de Brienne, when Brienne took charge of the French government in April 1787 and made a last, desperate effort to save the state as it was collapsing before the forces that led to the Revolution. Just as he had done during the ministry of Turgot, Morellet supplied Brienne with proposals, criticism, and preambles for edicts. His letters went out to Versailles every day. Brienne jotted responses in the margins, and they met on Fridays, going over all the issues, point by point, in long walks through the royal gardens.

To the revolutionaries, Brienne epitomized the evils of ministerial despotism. To Morellet, he was the last in the line of enlightened reformers that stretched back to Turgot, Trudaine, and Vincent de Gournay. He was the bright, young clergyman who had dreamed of a glorious career during their student days at the Maison de Sorbonne. He also was a *grand seigneur*. In one of the few lyrical passages of the memoirs, Morellet describes a visit to the magnificent château that Brienne and his brother had constructed on their family estate in Champagne. The estate had everything: vast hunting grounds, parks, terraces, pavilions, a theater, a ballroom, a huge library, a *cabinet d'histoire naturelle*, a *cabinet de physique* (complete with a demonstrator brought from Paris to amuse the ladies), "everything that can arouse interest, occupy people and distract them."[47] Morellet especially remembered the balls given by the Briennes in the summer. They set up tables and a dance floor in the gardens, brought in an orchestra from Paris, and invited all the best company from the neighboring countryside and the capital. There, as the wine flowed and the music played, Morellet improvised a song:

> Puisque ce séjour abonde
> En biens, en plaisirs si grands,

Revenons-y tous les ans
De tout autre lieu du monde;
J'y chanterai de nouveau,
Si votre voix me seconde,
J'y chanterai de nouveau
Et Brienne et son château.

Since this visit abounds
In good things, in such great pleasures,
Let us come back every year,
From every other part of the world;
Then I will sing again,
If you will agree,
To both Brienne and his château[48]

The abbé's singing to the lord of the manor calls up the refrain in *Le Mariage de Figaro*, Pierre-Augustin Caron de Beaumarchais's frothy satire of life during the last years of the ancien régime: "Everything finishes with songs." But Beaumarchais was wrong. It finished in a revolution.

A Career in the Middle Range: Baculard d'Arnaud

Morellet's success showed how an author could prosper from privileged positions, but the supply of privileges far exceeded the demand; and as the population of writers increased, fewer aspirants had access to the protection and patronage necessary to rise through the ranks. Those who failed to make it to the top often sank to the bottom or abandoned literature altogether, but some managed to survive in the middle range of the literary world. They included several well-known writers, such as Simon-Nicholas Henri Linguet, Charles Palissot, Louis Sébastien Mercier, Nicolas Restif de la Bretonne, and Jacques-Henri Bernardin de Saint-Pierre. Although they followed different paths, they had to cope with the same conditions, which can be appreciated by studying the career of a typical author from the middle range, François-Thomas Marie de Baculard d'Arnaud.[49]

Like Marmontel, d'Arnaud attempted to launch his career under the protection of Voltaire. Born in 1718 to a well-off Parisian family (his father acquired nobility by purchasing the office of secretary of the king but lost most of his fortune in the 1730s), he received a solid, classical education in the Jesuit Collège d'Harcourt. He took to writing poetry and plays as a schoolboy. At age seventeen, he sent Voltaire some verse full of flattery and enlightened sentiments, and received an encouraging letter in return. The correspondence grew, as d'Arnaud continued to send poems and Voltaire, who spent most of the years 1734–1749 with his mistress, the marquise of Châtelet, in Cirey, Champagne, employed the young man to run literary errands in Paris. By 1738, d'Arnaud had become a protégé. Voltaire rewarded him with small sums of money, and promised to find him "a position in which it is possible not to die of hunger"—that is, a sinecure.[50] An appointment connected with Helvétius, a wealthy tax farmer, fell through, but Voltaire arranged for d'Arnaud to become a literary correspondent of Frederick II, king of Prussia, a matter of supplying books and gossip for 1,000 L. a year. D'Arnaud published a good deal of incidental verse in the *Mercure* and a three-act tragedy, *Coligny*, about the massacre of Protestants on Saint Bartholomew's Day 1572.

Just when he seemed to be gaining a foothold in the literary world, however, d'Arnaud succumbed to a temptation faced by many writers who needed cash. He published a pornographic tract, *L'art de foutre, ou, Paris foutant* [The Art of fucking, or Fucking in Paris] (1741). The police, well informed about the speculation, packed him off to the Bastille and then to the prison of Saint-Lazare, which was normally used to punish dissolute youths and, unlike the Bastille, did not arouse sympathy for the victims of persecution.[51] After two months of confinement, d'Arnaud resumed his garret existence, still backed by Voltaire, who had no aversion to bawdy verse—far from it: he applauded his protégé's *Épître au cul de Manon* [Epistle to Manon's ass] (1748), which also delighted Frederick II. But this ephemera, along with a libertine novel, *Le Bal de Venise* (1747) and a privately performed play, *Le Mauvais Riche* (1750), did nothing to distinguish d'Arnaud from dozens of other obscure wits.

A turning point came with a court case of 1745, which d'Arnaud—and much of Paris—followed intensely.[52] Charles Huchet de La Bédoyère, a young aristocrat from an eminent Breton family, had fallen in love with an actress from the Comédie italienne, Agathe Sticotti. Instead of taking her as his mistress in the usual fashion of men about town, he married her, acting on his own without his parents' consent, because he knew they would disapprove. His father sued to get the marriage annulled, partly on technical grounds (lack of reference to the parents in the publication of the bans) and primarily because it was a monstrous *mésalliance*. Actors and actresses, however famous, did not belong to respectable society. Notorious for their immorality, they were not considered as Christians and could not take communion or be buried in sacred ground unless they renounced their profession. Charles, who was destined for a legal career, argued his own case. He and his wife had married because they loved one another, he insisted, and their union, consecrated by the church, could not be undone because his father objected to his wife's inferior status. Love should triumph over social prejudice. The lawyer for his father responded by defending marriage as a sacred institution embedded in the social order, one that bound families together and protected their honor by maintaining paternal authority. To treat marriage as a union of individuals based on nothing more than sentiment, he concluded, was to undermine the foundation of society. The court decided in favor of the father and declared the marriage illegitimate.

Deeply moved by Charles's defense, d'Arnaud transformed the judicial affair into a two-volume tale of love and suffering, *Les Époux malheureux* [The unhappy spouses] (1745). He presented the novel as a true story, narrated in the first person by Charles, but he barely mentioned the legal procedure. Instead, he concentrated on the innermost emotions of the young couple, elevating their love into a form of *sensibilité* (sensitivity) that eclipsed all social distinctions.

In the fictionalized version of their story, Charles and Agathe fall in love instantly and absolutely, then do everything possible to persuade Charles's father to permit them to marry. He, however, has arranged for Charles to wed a "young woman from a good family," who will bring him an income of 50,000 L. If Charles refuses, he will be disinherited, barred from the legal profession, and imprisoned by a *lettre de cachet* (a royal order for the imprisonment of a subject without any judicial procedure). An uncle comes to

Paris in an attempt to save the family's honor by persuading Charles to abandon Agathe, but Charles will not be moved, and his constancy, expressed in several tearful scenes, only makes Agathe aware that they are doomed by an insurmountable barrier of prejudice. She then decides to sacrifice herself. Having renounced the stage, she secretly leaves Paris to join a convent, accompanied by the uncle. They get as far as Mantes, where she succumbs to a nearly fatal case of heartbreak, lamenting "one is miserable to have such a sensitive heart."[53] Charles learns of her flight and tracks her down to the inn at Mantes. He appeals to his uncle's better nature: "Do not close your soul to this sensitivity that speaks to you for me."[54] By now, *sensibilité* has emerged as the force that is driving the plot. The uncle, moved by the beauty and virtue of Agathe and the "torrent of tears" that overcomes all three of them, agrees to try to persuade Charles's father to permit the marriage. Charles and Agathe return to Paris. After waiting in vain for a letter from the father, they take their fate in their own hands and get married without his consent.

From this point onward, d'Arnaud takes the reader through a succession of torments inflicted on the couple. Charles loses his case in court; they flee to Avignon to escape a *lettre de cachet*; disinherited and disbarred from a legal career, Charles cannot provide for the family; in desperation, Agathe offers to become a domestic servant, but Charles refuses to accept that ultimate dishonor; the *lettre de cachet* is withdrawn; and they return to Paris but only to sink deeper into poverty while Agathe becomes pregnant. Finally, Agathe leaves Charles and takes a position under an assumed name as a chambermaid to his mother, hoping to reveal her true identity once she has won over the parents by her virtuous behavior. She nearly succeeds, but a wicked priest intervenes; another *lettre de cachet* is issued; and Agathe returns to Paris, where she finds Charles mortally ill. With his last breath, Charles prays that the duke of Orléans will look after his wife and child, and the novel ends on a note of despair: true love has been defeated by the conventions of a heartless social order.

D'Arnaud managed to publish the novel by the end of 1745, when the La Bédoyère case was still fresh in the public's memory. At that time, *sensibilité* was beginning to be fashionable—and far more than a fashion, as d'Arnaud presented it: "It is sensitivity alone that makes us appreciate the price of existence."[55] He filled almost every scene in the book with "torrents of tears," and his readers loved it. *Les Époux malheureux* went through at least sixty editions, he later claimed (probably with some exaggeration). It became one of the top bestsellers in the eighteenth century, although it has since been forgotten and probably would be unreadable for most people today.[56]

There is little information about the payments d'Arnaud received from his publishers.[57] Like most writers, he probably settled for relatively small sums in exchange for his manuscripts and never collected anything more, except when he reworked the texts for new editions. Royalties did not exist, and most of the subsequent editions were pirated. But the success of *Les Époux malheureux* brought d'Arnaud recognition as a writer. In addition to his services for Frederick II, he became literary correspondent to the Duke of Wurttemberg, a position worth another 1,000 L. a year, and in March 1750 Frederick invited him to Berlin. French writers often added luster to their careers by spending time in foreign courts. They contributed a fashionable French touch to court life while improving their own prestige and fortune. By inviting d'Arnauld, Frederick, a francophile, increased the supply of Gallic wit in his entourage, and he also hoped to lure Voltaire, who had resisted many invitations but was vulnerable to jealousy. Once Frederic hinted at the possibility of d'Arnauld becoming his favorite, Voltaire resolved to take up residence in Potsdam-Berlin as chamberlain to the philosopher-king and the leading light of his academy.

Of course, d'Arnauld could not pretend to be a rival of the most famous writer in Europe, and Frederick gave Voltaire a very warm welcome when he finally arrived in July 1750. But several minor incidents, including some compromising correspondence between d'Arnauld and Voltaire's enemy Fréron, provoked Voltaire to turn against the young man he had once protected. He persuaded Frederick to expel d'Arnauld, who sought refuge in Dresden, where he had connections with the Saxon court. But a pension failed to materialize, d'Arnauld's finances collapsed, and in June 1754 he was back in Paris, reduced to living by his pen.

For the next fifty years, nearly up to the time of his death in 1805, d'Arnauld churned out books. He also produced poetry, plays, and ephemera on all sorts of subjects, but he relied primarily on the genre that had made *Les Époux malheureux* such a success, novels built on *sensibilité*. The same themes constantly reappeared: pure love thwarted by social convention, self-sacrifice by virtuous heroines, despair by overpowered heroes, and unbearable suffering, all of it drenched in tears.

Fanny, the first in a series of novelettes that d'Arnaud published from 1764 to 1780, combined these ingredients in a typical tale, set in England and inspired by Richardson's *Pamela*. Lord Thaley, a young aristocrat with a weak will but a good heart, encounters Fanny, the beautiful and virtuous daughter of a farmer on one of his estates. They immediately fall in love and plan to marry, but Thaley's father opposes the misalliance. Sir Thoward, an evil companion of Thaley, pretends to solve the problem by concocting a secret wedding, which takes place but in fact is invalid. Thoward then entices Thaley to take up a corrupt life in London, leaving Fanny on the farm. Thaley's father arranges for him to marry an aristocratic heiress, and while they indulge in the pleasures of high society, Fanny and her father sink into poverty. After several twists in the plot—the death of the heiress-wife, a duel, and Thaley's spiritual awakening—the original lovers are united, shedding "those sweet tears that escape from the soul." Thaley has learned that "sentiment must triumph over all prejudice," and they live happily ever after.[58]

Fanny succeeded so well that d'Arnaud followed it up with another sentimental novel, *Sidnei et Silli* (1766); then another, *Nancy* (1767); and another, *Lucie et Mélanie* (1767); and so on, twenty-five in all, up to *Amélie* (1780). After publishing them separately, he revised them and combined them in various editions, which came to be known by a common title, *Les Épreuves du sentiment* (The trials of sentiment). D'Arnauld negotiated arrangements with five different publishers during the sixteen years when he cranked out the texts. How much he made cannot be determined. It probably was enough for him to live in some comfort, although the publishers did not give him a share in the income from their sales. In 1782, he complained that a twenty-five-volume edition "produced twenty thousand livres for the publisher and not a penny for me."[59]

While laboring on *Les Épreuves du sentiment*, d'Arnaud began a similar run of novelettes, *Nouvelles historiques*, published individually and in different combinations from 1774 to 1784. The full series included eight works, which were as sentimental as the *Épreuves* but were set in the Middle Ages and appealed to a vogue for the lugubrious and the gothic, which had also arrived from England. *Salisbury*, the first of the collection, takes place in the fourteenth century. Alix, the beautiful and dutiful daughter of Lord Varuccy, marries the Count of Salisbury, but is secretly in love with King Edward III, who is also smitten with her, although for political reasons he is committed to wed the Princess of Haynaut. Alix sacrifices herself by withdrawing to a convent after her husband dies. The king is seized with despair: "He paced around; he turned his eyes to the sky; he became furious; he let out a kind of howling; he collapsed on a chair; and then he poured a torrent of tears onto the ground."[60] In the end, they accept their fate.

Before the last of the *Nouvelles historiques* had appeared, d'Arnaud launched yet another series, *Délassements de l'homme sensible* (Diversions of a sensitive man) (1783–1786), which ran to twelve volumes comprising twenty-four parts. He built his tales around reports about heroism and suffering, which he culled from various journals or simply invented. While the tears flowed as abundantly as ever, the tone of the narratives became darker. D'Arnaud explained in a preface that he had adopted "the tenebrous genre" in order to get across the depths of *sensibilité*. Sorrow now became bathetic,

misery turned into melancholia, and moralizing gave way
to despair. In *Norston et Suzanne, ou le malheur*, for example,
a virtuous couple fights off poverty in colonial New York.
While their children are dying of starvation, their creditors
threaten them with debtors' prison. Norston abandons hope.
"You see," he confesses to Suzanne, "what my sensitivity has
reduced me to, to pierce your heart, you and your children!
We are lost without the slightest support!"[61] Jonathan, a
black-hearted villain, tempts Suzanne with a bag of coins
in exchange for sex. She indignantly refuses, but then faints
and is raped. When she regains consciousness, she finds
the bag at her feet. Desperate to feed her children, she pur-
chases some bread, but, unknown to her, the coins turn out
to be fake. The couple are thrown into prison, then brought
to trial as counterfeiters. With her last ounce of strength,
Suzanne delivers an eloquent speech exposing Jonathan's
wickedness. She collapses and dies; Norston commits suicide; Jonathan is hanged; and the story ends on a note of
desolation.

Whereas the earlier works had sold well and went
through edition after edition, *Délassements d'un homme sensible* failed to please the public. D'Arnaud tried to publish it
by subscription so that he could keep the sales for himself,
but apparently he cleared next to nothing and discontinued
the series after 1786. By this time, he was reduced to poverty. He inherited little, if anything, when his father died in
1757, and he probably gained little in the way of a dowry
in 1770, when he married a saleswoman who gave birth to
a son.[62] For a while in the 1760s, he collected a small pension on the *Mercure*, and in 1781 he gained a position as
secretary to the count of Artois, which brought in 1,200 L.

a year. How long he collected that income is unclear, but unlike Marmontel, he did not support himself with pensions and sinecures. He survived by writing—endless writing in many genres, poems, plays, essays, short stories, novels— and selling every scrap that his publishers would take. He wrote so much and recycled it so often that his output can only be estimated. His prose fiction included more than fifty separate works, many of them containing several volumes.[63] Judging from the many reprints and pirated editions, the books that went over best were the tales of *sensibilité*, which capitalized on the success of *Les Époux malheureux*. D'Arnaud had found a formula that worked, and he flogged it for all it was worth until the 1780s, when he had exhausted its appeal.

The appeal apparently extended to a general and rel- atively unsophisticated public, although one can only speculate about the identity of d'Arnauld's readers and their responses. Grimm claimed that no one in the social and intellectual elite paid any attention to d'Arnauld's works: "I am persuaded that the salesgirls in the rue des Lombards and the rue des Bourdonnais, who are full of sentiment, find the novels of M. d'Arnaud very beautiful and that his pathetic pen makes them weep abundant tears," he com- mented sardonically. "In the provinces this must also seem very touching, but in the neighborhood of the Palais-Royal and in the faubourg Saint-Germain, I am the only one who knows that M. d'Arnaud writes novels."[64] Of course, Grimm wrote as an ally of the philosophes, and after his quarrel with Voltaire, d'Arnauld had become identified with their opponents. Fréron, Voltaire's archenemy, reviewed d'Ar- naud's works enthusiastically in the *Année littéraire*. Partisans of the Enlightenment shed "sweet tears" like everyone else in the late eighteenth century, but they did not respond to d'Arnauld's version of sensitivity. His sentimental moralizing represented a break with the worldly, witty tone of his early writing, to say nothing of the libertinism in *L'art de foutre* and *Épître au cul de Manon*. His publications after 1750 did not contain the slightest criticism of the church or the established social order, even though he deplored the suffering inflicted by the powerful on the weak.[65] All of his books in the last decades of the ancien régime were published with privileges or tacit permissions. He never had any difficulty with the censors.

In fact, d'Arnauld kept a low profile after he returned to Paris from Germany, and he spent most of his last years scribbling in obscurity. He earned enough to support his family, but he relied heavily on loans, which he rarely repaid. He borrowed from everyone, taking whatever he could get, often only a few *écus* (coins worth 3 L.). According to Chamfort, he begged for so many *écus* from so many acquaintances that their total value amounted to 300,000 L. When he failed to return a loan from Necker, d'Arnauld explained that he was laboring under "more distress than words can tell," and he asked for 1,200 L. more—or at least 700 L., "because misery oppresses me and is at its worst." Necker wrote in a margin of the letter, "Sent four louis. [96 L.]"[66]

Having tried and failed to get ahead by cultivating patrons and collecting pensions and sinecures—the strategy that carried Morellet to the top—d'Arnauld proved that a writer could live by his pen. It took talent and enormous labor, but his relative success showed that it was possible, barely, for someone located in the middle range of the literary world to survive, provided he could find a niche in the book market and make the most of it.

Down and Out in Literary Paris: Pierre-Louis Manuel

While Baculard d'Arnaud scraped together enough income to survive in the middle ranks of the literary world, Pierre-Louis Manuel eked out an existence at the bottom. Paris was full of hack writers, the "poor devils" derided by Voltaire who lived by all sorts of expedients—occasional stints as tutors, correcting proof in printing shops, scribbling articles for underground gazettes, churning out libels and pornography, pamphleteering, peddling, and sometimes spying for the police. The hacks performed so many odd jobs that their careers did not conform to a single pattern. What they had in common was poverty—and in most cases resentment against the system that drove them into hack work. Many began like d'Arnaud, full of ambition to follow Voltaire's path to honor and glory. They ended like Manuel, frustrated, bitter, and eager to throw themselves into a new system as soon as the Revolution destroyed the old.[67]

Manuel lived in such obscurity before 1789 that it is difficult to reconstruct his career, but the surviving evidence shows that, like many writers, his first steps led through the church.[68] He was born in 1753 and grew up in Montargis, where his father had a retail cloth business. He did so well in a local school taught by Barnabite monks that his parents sent him to a seminary in Sens, hoping he would become a priest. But according to a hostile tract from 1793, *Vie secrète de Pierre Manuel*, he adopted the views of a Voltairean and the airs of a fop who frequented the local literati and chased after women. He left the seminar after two years, traveled to Paris to handle some business for his father, spent all the money he collected, and after he ran out of funds joined the Parisian Séminaire Saint-Louis, where he rose to be an instructor ("maître des conférences"). He sprinkled his lessons with so much irreligion, however, that he was expelled. Then as a militant partisan of the philosophes, he resolved to seek his fortune in the world of letters. He supported himself by various teaching positions, including a stint as a tutor in the house of a banker named Tourton, but he was dismissed after being denounced for impiety, and eventually fell back on employment in the printing shop of J. B. Garnery, a Parisian bookseller.[69] In return for a free room and occasional payments, he corrected proof, procured manuscripts, and distributed pamphlets to peddlers.

Manuel also cobbled together odd jobs in the illegal sector of the book trade, as we will see. Meanwhile, he attempted to make a name for himself by publishing poems, epigrams, and essays in periodicals like the *Mercure* and the *Journal encyclopédique*. He collected several of them in a volume of miscellany, *Essais historiques, critiques, littéraires et philosophiques par M. Man . . .* (1783). The essays give the impression of a young writer exhibiting his talent and signaling his commitment to the cause of the philosophes. They celebrated the genius of Buffon, d'Alembert, and especially Voltaire; and they included irreverent remarks about religious prejudice, but nothing so outspoken as to cause difficulties with the censors, who permitted the book to appear with a tacit permission. Manuel served up anecdotes about all sorts of subjects—the wisdom of the ancients, current hair styles among Parisian women, the importance of agriculture, the excessive wealth of monasteries, the place of virtue in pedagogy, the valor of Maria Theresa of Austria, historic sites in Paris. They had a belletristic flavor and included some fiction ("Les Amours de Fatime et d'Almanzor," a short story with an Oriental motif), but they were not tied together by any common themes and were weighed down by clichés ("The masterpiece of love is the heart of a mother"). One essay seemed to evoke Manuel's own experience. Parents should steer their children away from "the career of letters," he warned. Young men frequently took a little talent to be genius and set out to conquer Parnassus: "Barely out of school, a young man wants to speak the language of the gods. First it is a quatrain to be posted on the statue of a long-haired Jupiter, then a madrigal for the bust of an *actrice*, . . . then a song against prelates, an epigram against husbands, a *logogriphe* (word puzzle), a drama, and perhaps a delicious tragedy." But no amount of effort was likely to open access to a successful career in the overcrowded world of letters.[70] The *Essais historiques* did not provide an entry point for Manuel. Judging from literary journals and the *Correspondance littéraire* of Grimm and La Harpe, it was never reviewed and probably not noticed.

Manuel tried again to win recognition as a man of letters with a Voltairean volume, *Coup d'oeil philosophique sur le règne de Saint-Louis* (1786). As in Voltaire's *Essai sur les moeurs*, it deplored the ignorance and superstition of the Middle Ages, especially the barbarism of the crusades. Manuel held high "the flame of philosophy" to expose abuses by the church. Yet he again abstained from saying anything critical enough to provoke the censors, who allowed the book to be sold openly with Manuel's name on the title page. Louis IX's piety and his role as leader of the seventh and eighth crusades posed a problem for Manuel, who maintained an anticlerical tone throughout the book. He resolved it by celebrating Louis as a statesman rather than a saint: "He gave the first signal of liberty to the population." Manuel did not support this remark with any evidence. In fact, he provided only a thin narrative and then cut it short because, as he announced at the end, he had learned that a large-scale work was about to be published on the same subject.[71] In a brief review, Grimm dismissed the book as derivative from Voltaire and written in "a constantly declamatory tone that is often completely unintelligible."[72]

While failing to make his mark as an essayist and historian, Manuel turned out hack work. *Lettre d'un garde du roi pour servir de suite aux Mémoires de Cagliostro* (Letter by a guard of the king to serve as a sequel to the *Mémoires of Cagliostro*) (1786) was an anonymous, thirty-four-page pamphlet designed to satisfy the public's hunger for anything related to the Diamond Necklace Affair. On August 15, 1785, the cardinal de Rohan was arrested for attempting to win the queen's favor at a midnight rendezvous by presenting her with a diamond necklace, supposedly worth 1.6 million L. In fact, the cardinal was duped by some swindlers, who sold off the diamonds after hiring a prostitute to play the part of the queen and staging the meeting in the gardens of Versailles. While trying to unravel a complicated conspiracy, the authorities filled the Bastille with suspects. Their biggest prize, or the one who most fascinated the public, was Joseph Balsamo, an Italian adventurer who called himself Count Cagliostro and claimed to have found the secret of avoiding death by gaining access to the wisdom of the ancient Egyptians. Cagliostro actually had nothing to do with the diamond necklace swindle, but he had ingratiated himself with Rohan and was arrested under suspicion of being Rohan's accomplice.

Before the trial, which eventually found them both to be innocent, Cagliostro defended himself and stoked the public's interest in his extravagant career by publishing some judicial memoirs ("factums" or legal briefs, which could circulate openly provided they carried the name of a lawyer). They sold spectacularly, and Manuel tried to capitalize on their success by presenting his pamphlet as a commentary on them made by one of the king's guards, who discussed every aspect of the affair with the salty common sense of a man of the people. Thanks to his guard duties, he had seen the king and ministers up close. He had no illusions concerning *les grands*, yet he spoke respectfully about them and even maintained that the Bastille was a necessary evil, because prisons were essential to a well governed state. He treated Rohan as a dupe and Cagliostro as a confidence man but neither as guilty of a crime. In fact, the guard did not assign any guilt at all. Instead, he concluded that the whole affair was unfathomable: "Everything is bizarre, the motives, the means, the personages."[73]

Despite this unobjectionable conclusion, the police set out to confiscate every copy of *Lettre d'un garde du roi* and all the other pamphlets about the Diamond Necklace Affair. The scandal had compromised the honor of the queen, and the government was determined to stifle public discussion of it. On January 31, 1786, the police discovered a cache of the

Lettre in the Palais-Royal bookshop of Edme-Marie-Pierre Desauges, a notorious dealer in forbidden books. Desauges said he had acquired his copies from Manuel. Three days later, the police raided Manuel's apartment, confiscated his papers, and carried him off to the Bastille. They kept him two months and interrogated him six times.[74]

In the first interrogation, the lieutenant general of police accused him of being the author of the *Lettre*. Manuel, who identified himself as a "man of letters," denied that he had written it but admitted that he had handled the distribution of the edition, which came to 1,000 copies. He refused to reveal the names of the pamphlet's author and printer because, he said, it was against his principles to compromise anyone. In the second interrogation, Manuel replied that he actually was the author but considered himself innocent, as the pamphlet contained nothing seditious: "It was only a commercial speculation." He had merely hoped to cash in on the demand for everything connected with Cagliostro's memoirs. In the third interrogation, Manuel reversed himself again, claiming that he had not written the pamphlet after all, and he stood firm in his refusal to provide information about its printing. The record of Manuel's last three interrogations has disappeared, but a note in the dossier indicated that he had cracked under cross examination on February 16 and revealed that the *Lettre* had been written by his friend, a hack writer named Charles-Joseph Mayer, and printed by Jean Augustin Grangé, a seventy-three-year-old specialist in the underground book trade.

Manuel provided more details in a written confession, which he sent to the lieutenant general of police. In a conversation about the astonishing sales of Cagliostro's memoirs, he explained, he and Mayer had marveled that a cheap brochure could bring in more revenue than a serious book. "Well then," he said to Mayer, "write one, and provided that it does not compromise anyone, I will handle the rest. The cost will be covered by me and the profit will be for the two of us."[75] Although the police never got their hands on Mayer, they arrested several others connected with the speculation: two printers, two bookdealers, and a peddler, all of them veterans of the illegal book trade. After interrogating the prisoners and combing through Manuel's papers, the police uncovered a whole series of clandestine publishing ventures, with Manuel at the heart of them.

The papers included a small account book in which Manuel recorded sales he had made of libels, pornography, and other works to booksellers, peddlers, and individual customers. His correspondence showed that he ordered the books from foreign publishers (Dufour of Maastricht, Barde of Geneva, Dujardin of Brussels) who specialized in producing works that were prohibited in France. Manuel published some forbidden books himself—small editions, which could be run off on clandestine presses in Paris for only a few hundred livres and distributed "under the cloak" by peddlers. To operate this micropublishing business, Manuel dealt with shady characters who were familiar to the police—Desauges, Grangé, a peddler turned printer named François Normand, and Louis Dupré, a former wigmaker who took up clandestine printing under the alias "Point." Manuel also acted as a middleman, selling manuscripts to the foreign publishers and manuscript gazettes ("nouvelles à la main") to various customers.

One dossier revealed that Manuel's business included a great many transactions with Mirabeau and especially Mirabeau's mistress, Henriette-Amélie de Nehra, who managed some of his affairs in 1785 and 1786.[76] It contained notes by the police on letters from Mme de Nehra to Manuel instructing him to arrange for the publication of several works by Mirabeau. At this time Mirabeau, helped by a team of hack writers, was producing a series of pamphlets that denounced stock jobbing ("agiotage") on the Bourse, particularly speculations on futures by financiers who bet on a bear market. By exposing inflated stock, the pamphlets were intended to provoke a drop in the market that would benefit Mirabeau's backers among bear speculators. The bulls replied with pamphlets of their own, and the polemics soon attracted a large readership. In his interrogations, Manuel admitted that he had arranged the printing and distribution of four of the Mirabeau works. Although they were produced outside the law, the government had permitted them to circulate, so Manuel's admission did not expose him to punishment; and the police were intent on tracing works connected with the Diamond Necklace Affair, so they did not pursue the lead about Mirabeau. But they noted that seven of the letters to Manuel "announced that M. de Mirabeau had withdrawn confidence in him; there are even some bitter reproaches and hard words." A letter from Mme de Nerha made clear that after sending several manuscripts for Manuel to print, she suspected him of secretly arranging for a pirated edition of *Lettre du comte de Mirabeau à M. le Couteulx de la Noraye sur la Banque de Saint-Charles et sur la Caisse d'Escompte* (Brussels, 1785) and keeping the profits for himself. The dossier contained a bill from a printer who had run off five hundred copies of that pamphlet for Manuel at a cost of 300 L. Evidently, Manuel had double-crossed Mirabeau while serving as his agent.

Although Manuel asserted his identity as a man of letters, his interrogations in the Bastille show that he supported himself as a small-scale entrepreneur in the underground book trade. He sold forbidden books, arranged for their printing, and operated as a middleman in all sorts of speculations. Owing to his immersion in this milieu, he had a great deal of information that he could provide to the police. Their record of his interrogations does not contain a detailed report of what he revealed to them, and the account he himself published in *La Bastille dévoilée*, a selection from the Bastille archives made available to him after its destruction in 1789, says very little.[77] But two items in the papers of Jean-Charles-Pierre Lenoir, lieutenant general of police from August 1774 to May 1775 and from June 1776 to August 1785, say a great deal about the company he kept. The first is an undated report by a police inspector on Pierre-Jean Audouin, a hack pamphleteer who would become a radical journalist and Jacobin during the Revolution. It said that Audouin lived by peddling forbidden books in association with Manuel and other "bad writers." The second is a reference by Lenoir to an underground publishing business run by Marc Antoine Sanson: "Manuel, a writer and peddler who then worked as a salaried spy for a police inspector, said in a denunciation that he had seen obscene works turned out by Sanson's printing shop and kept by Sanson in a clandestine warehouse by the Hôtel du Contrôle des finances."[78]

Was Manuel a police spy? Lenoir's testimony must be read with skepticism, because he composed it sometime after fleeing Paris in 1789, when he felt nothing but hostility to the Revolution and its leaders. As already mentioned, he made the same claim about Brissot, a close friend of Manuel who also took up journalism and radical politics after struggling to survive in the bottom ranks of the literary world. For my part, I find Lenoir's revelations convincing, although they cannot be confirmed with absolute certainty.[79]

Despite his connections with the literary underground, Manuel did not abandon his ambition to make a name for himself as an author. At the end of 1788 he published a four-volume work, *L'Année française, ou vies des hommes qui ont honoré la France, ou par leurs talents, ou par leurs services, et surtout par leurs vertus* (The French year, or lives of men who have honored France by their talents or by their services and especially by their virtues). In a preface, he explained that the inspiration for it had come to him while suffering as an innocent prisoner in the Bastille. He had worked on it for the following two years, determined, he said, to promote civic virtue by celebrating the lives of great men. He attached a biographical sketch of a great man's life to each day of the year so that the book could serve as an educational almanac. By reading an entry every day to their children, fathers would form virtuous citizens, and teachers would do the same in readings before their pupils. Conventional almanacs were cheap chapbooks, which linked the names of saints to each day. In contrast to them, Manuel celebrated secular heroes, especially among the common people: "Far from me the idea of celebrating those sovereigns who merely were powerful and valorous. I seek out citizens whose knowledge, talents, and virtues have honored my fatherland."[80] In fact, however, *L'Année française* was a scissors-and-paste job, which Manuel cobbled together from other works, and it received no attention from reviewers.

Manuel himself finally attracted some attention in 1788, but of the worst sort—one sentence in *Le Petit Almanach de nos grands-hommes* (1788), a sarcastic send-up (to be discussed later) of minor men of letters by Antoine Rivarol: "Manuel. An amiable and facile Muse who is capable of everything but prefers to win immortality by following the dainty paths of madrigals and epigrams."[81] Deeply wounded, Manuel replied in a pamphlet: "According to you, M. Manuel would be capable of producing an epic poem because he does madrigals—Manuel, who with more philosophy than fortune devotes himself in obscurity to useful work! You denounce him as a maker of epigrams! No such gall has ever poisoned his heart."[82] Rivarol retorted with another pamphlet, which scorned Manuel as an example of the "riff raff" from the "swamp of Parnassus" that had flooded France's literary scene.[83] By this time Manuel was reduced to correcting proof and distributing pamphlets to peddlers in Garnery's printing shop. A biographical sketch of him in the *Dictionnaire des Conventionnels* concluded, "At the outbreak of the Revolution he was poor and bitter."[84]

THE FACTS OF
LITERARY LIFE

ANY ATTEMPT TO produce an overview of France's literary population runs into problems of definitions and sources. Should anyone whose work has appeared in print deserve to be considered as a writer, or should the notion of a writer be restricted to those who published in certain genres or depended on writing for a living or merely identified themselves as among the *gens de lettres*? One way to negotiate around this difficulty is to adopt a criterion that was favored in the eighteenth century, arbitrary though it may be—that anyone who has published at least one book may be considered a writer. That was the definition used in *La France littéraire*, a guide to writers and writing published at regular intervals throughout the second half of the eighteenth century. *La France littéraire* provides the only way to study France's literary population, short of recruiting a team of researchers to run a dragnet through all available biographies and bibliographies, whether online or out of sight in ancient card catalogs. It began as an almanac, small enough to fit into a waistcoat pocket, and developed into a multivolume biographical dictionary. In the course of its evolution through a dozen editions and supplements, it became a fixture of literary life, a kind of Who's Who consulted by anyone who wanted to locate anyone else within the French republic of letters. It has defects, of course. As a census it is amateurish, as a bibliography incomplete. But it improved as it grew from edition to edition, so that by 1757 it had become remarkably comprehensive.[1]

La France littéraire

The book first appeared in 1752 under the title *Almanach des beaux-arts*. It contained only thirty-five leaves without pagination. Its author, François-Joachim Duport du Tertre, a Jesuit turned hack writer, followed the format of the pocket almanacs popular at that time. He listed the movable feast days, then included a calendar with notes on the days of saints, and finally gave the names of notable figures in the beaux-arts and sister disciplines, 321 in all, of whom 176 might be considered writers. It was a slapdash job, but it met with some success, because du Tertre came back the next year with a new edition three times the size of the first. He announced that any authors he had overlooked would be included in future editions if they informed the publisher, N. B. Duchesne, of their names and works.

In 1755 the book reappeared under a new title, *La France littéraire*. Although still an almanac, it now ran to 240 pages and contained notices on 726 "gens de lettres." The edition of 1756 was still bigger. A great many writers had sent in letters identifying themselves and their works, du Tertre explained in the preface. He encouraged every author in France to do the same. It was their book, and so he dedicated it to them: "à Messieurs les auteurs." Anyone who had published a book was entitled to an entry. If enough writers collaborated in the enterprise, *La France littéraire* would include all of literary France.[2]

By 1757 it probably had come close to that goal. The preface of that year's edition indicated that letters had arrived from every corner of France with lists of all the local writers. For example, Father Rozet, a Dominican monk and an energetic member of the Société littéraire de Besançon, received a grateful acknowledgment for supplying notices on every author in the Franche-Comté. His own contribution to literature was a very minor work, *Examen de la cause de la chute de l'Eglise des Jacobins de Besançon* (Examination of the cause of the collapse of the Jacobin Church in Besançon). Clearly *La France littéraire* had penetrated deep into the world of the provincial literati. It now covered 1,187 writers and made clear that it would exclude those who did not qualify—that is, those who had published the occasional essay or poem in a literary review but did not count as full-fledged writers because they had never published a book.

The new emphasis on comprehensiveness bore the mark of the book's new author, Joseph de La Porte, who took over from du Tertre in mid-1756. No one considered La Porte as anything more than a hack writer, but he was an extraordinarily diligent hack. He compiled and anthologized more than anyone else in that golden age of scissors-and-paste publishing. An ex-Jesuit like du Tertre, he went down in the police files as a somewhat suspicious character: "He is a man who keeps bad company. He has been a Jesuit for eight

years and is a good friend of abbé Raynal. He is the com-
petitor of Fréron [Élie-Catherine Fréron, editor of _L'Année
littéraire_] and like him produces critical works in the genre
established by abbé Fontaines. He sells them himself and
has only that as a source of support."[3]

In literary circles, La Porte was known as a "tireless
compiler" and as "the echo of the Encyclopedists" in his
journalistic writing.[4] But whatever the company he kept
and the orthodoxy of his opinions, La Porte was a man who
could get the job done. He put together at least 214 volumes,
on all sorts of subjects from the commerce of the Chinese
to the manners of Englishwomen in the course of his long
literary career. One of the few writers who actually lived
by his pen, he was said to make between 6,000 and 12,000
livres a year. Not that he wrote much of what he saw into
print. "The important thing is not to write but to publish," he
reportedly remarked.[5] La Porte was the ideal person to take
du Tertre's almanac, give it a good shaking, turn it inside out,
and remake it as a large-scale reference work.

After maintaining du Tertre's format in the edition of
1757, La Porte issued his new model in 1758. He dropped
the calendar and other vestiges of the old almanac, including the subtitle, and organized the text into three parts: (1)
a list of all the academies, provincial and Parisian, with the
names of their members; (2) biographical notices on all
living French authors—that is, everyone he could identify
who had published a book; and (3) a short title list of all the
authors' works. _La France littéraire_ now provided a coherent
and remarkably broad view of French literature.

La Porte put out supplements in 1760, 1762, and 1764;
and in 1766 he decided to combine all the material he

had accumulated in a gigantic new edition. By then, however, he had taken on so many other compilations that he jobbed out much of the work to a friend, Jacques Hébrail, another ex-priest turned hack writer. The two men combed through literary reviews and La Porte's files, and in 1769 they turned out the most exhaustive *France littéraire* yet. It had increased in size from duodecimo to octavo and from one to two volumes. It included a new section of obituaries on authors who had died since 1751. And it covered 2,367 living authors, twice the number in the edition of 1757. Although La Porte continued to churn out compilations on other subjects and dropped Hébrail, he issued a supplement in 1778, claiming to have achieved greater coverage than ever.[6] He died a year later at the age of sixty-one. Having published enough to fill a small library, he renounced a great deal of it in a deathbed confession to an anti-Enlightenment priest.

A final version of *La France littéraire* appeared in 1784, compiled by Joseph-André Guiot, a clergyman and librarian in the Abbaye de Saint Victor in Paris. Guiot produced a fairly substantial new volume and added a new section entitled "Topographie de la France littéraire," which made it possible to follow the geographical distribution of authorship, or at least of authors' birthplaces. He announced his resolve to devote special attention to beginners, so that no writer, no matter how obscure, would disappear from the Republic of Letters without leaving a trace. But Guiot seemed to lack La Porte's energy with scissors and paste. His book looks thin in comparison with its predecessors. It demonstrates nonetheless that the literary population had reached an unprecedented size. If one combines entries from the supplements going back to 1769 and allows for deaths, *La France littéraire* indicates that France contained 2,819 writers on the eve of the Revolution—and it probably missed a great many of them.

How many? Unfortunately, one cannot measure the margin of error. The authors' assurances about the excellence of their work cannot be taken at face value, especially as it received mixed reviews from their contemporaries. Friedrich Melchior Grimm's *Correspondance littéraire* objected to the book's "innumerable mistakes" in 1762, and in 1778 an anonymous correspondent of the *Journal de Paris* compiled an embarrassingly long list of errors in its citations of titles and its attributions of authorship.[7] Yet the criticism concerned details of bibliography rather than comprehensiveness of coverage. Once it had shaken off its early existence as an almanac, *La France littéraire* was taken seriously as a standard reference work, even by Voltaire, who pretended to despise compilations. When La Porte first appealed to him for help in writing his notice, Voltaire did not deign to reply. But when the notice was published with titles of works that Voltaire had written but did not want to acknowledge, he was horrified. He fired off protests followed by a draft of the article as he wanted it to appear in future editions. *La France littéraire* was a force to be reckoned with, he confided to his niece: "It's a book that serves as a reference work, because it contains entries on all the academies in the kingdom, on all living authors in alphabetical order, and on all of their works."[8] La Porte had stressed the same theme in his prefaces. Any writer who wanted recognition had to take account of his appearance in *La France littéraire*.

At the same time, *La France littéraire* provided testimony to the improved status of writers in general. In 1762 it proclaimed triumphantly,

> France has never supplied a larger number of citizens to the Republic of Letters than in the current century. Among nearly eighteen hundred authors who appear in *La France littéraire* there are those from both sexes, from all occupations and positions, from that of a monarch to that of an artisan, thus demonstrating that membership in the world of letters does not degrade the highest dignities and does not exclude those from the lower ranks of society.[9]

The whole history of the book and even its form—from the biographical notices to the obituaries and the "literary topography"—demonstrate the growing importance of writers and of literature itself in the second half of the eighteenth century.

An Assessment

A vexing question remains, however: Does the increase in the number of biographical notices in the successive editions of *La France littéraire* correspond to an increase in the number of writers or to an improvement in the coverage of them? Clearly both elements contributed to the expansion of the book between 1752 and 1784, but what was their relative importance? I confess that I do not have an answer to that problem. But it seems likely that the improvement in the collection of data had leveled off by 1757, when La

Porte produced his first edition. By then, having incorporated the information in the earlier editions, he was able to
compile more, and the writers had had plenty of opportunity
to answer the appeals for notices about themselves. So, the
1,187 writers listed in the edition of 1757, including those
from the earlier editions and discounting for deaths and rep-
etitions, probably provide a fairly accurate idea of France's
literary population at midcentury.

Though La Porte and his collaborators had settled on
their definition of a writer, they did not define their notion
of a book. However, judging from the titles that appear in *La
France littéraire*, their implicit concept of a "book" extended
to some works that would be considered rather ephemeral
today. For them, therefore, literary France included a great
many obscure men of letters—priests who published their
sermons, small town doctors who turned out tracts on dis-
eases, and members of provincial academies who put their
discourses into print.[10] Far from favoring the glamorous
authors of Paris, *La France littéraire* gave plenty of space to
the intellectual world of the provinces, which had flourished
with the spread of academies and reading societies during
the first half of the century.[11]

This intellectual activity moved into a new phase after
1750. Inspired by the example of Voltaire and other famous
authors, new generations broke into print. They swelled the
ranks of the writers in *La France littéraire* of 1769 and the
supplement of 1778, and they probably would have increased
the size of the edition of 1784 had it been prepared more
thoroughly. But it was so deficient that booksellers considered producing a rival edition. A Parisian publisher named
Le Grand proposed to lift all the material from Guiot's

text, which he wrongly attributed to La Porte, and to supply enough information from other sources to satisfy the demand for a truly comprehensive work. Although it never came to fruition, the plan illustrates the way *La France littéraire* was viewed by professional bookmen on the eve of the Revolution.[12]

Fortunately, one can compensate for the deficiencies of the 1784 edition by extrapolating from the earlier editions and supplements.[13] The total then comes to 2,819, and one can calculate the growth in the number of writers as follows:

Table 2.1. Number of known writers, 1757–1784.

1757	1769	1784
1,187	2,367	2,819

I believe those figures represent the best estimate of France's literary population during the second half of the eighteenth century. The figure for 1784 is probably much too low, for it seems unlikely that the number of writers should have increased by 1,180 during the twelve years between 1757 and 1769 and by only 452 during the fifteen years between 1769 and 1784. The general population increased a great deal (even if the rate of growth dropped off after 1770) during the last four decades of the ancien régime, and the growing prestige of literature probably drew more young people into it, especially after 1778, when the deaths of Voltaire and Rousseau touched off a new wave of enthusiasm for the cult of the philosophe. I think it safe to conclude that by 1789 France had at least 3,000 writers, more than twice the number in 1750.[14]

Three thousand writers in a nation of twenty-six million about to explode in a revolution—do the figures suggest the existence of an inflammable intelligentsia?[15] Not in themselves, but they add a new dimension to Alexis de Tocqueville's emphasis on the importance of men of letters as a disruptive element in the ancien régime.[16] Louis-Sébastien Mercier went further, claiming that they shared a common, rebellious spirit, despite their divisions:

> Although not united among themselves, they agree on essential principles. They stigmatize the supporters of arbitrary power, recognize them under their disguises, denounce them and punish them. . . . They [men of letters] often produce a unanimous protest, which becomes the expression of universal reason. What can the established power do against this powerful voice? . . . It does everything possible to divide this body, which has the same spirit though it lacks a rallying point.[17]

Had poets become the unacknowledged legislators of the world before Percy Bysshe Shelley bestowed that title upon them? One should make allowances for Mercier's rhetoric and also for the tendency of authors to fight one another over all sorts of subjects, from free versus regulated trade to German versus Italian music. Their divisions deepened as the demographic pressure rose from 1750 to 1790, and this tendency undermined the ideological stability of the regime in a way that had nothing to do with "universal reason." It reinforced the growth of a particularly dangerous species of writer: the hack. The literary marketplace could not support three thousand writers. It probably could not support more than three dozen. As we have seen from the preceding case studies, authors who lacked an independent income generally relied on sinecures and pensions dispensed by protectors and patrons. But those favors remained in short supply while the demand for them kept increasing. The upper tier of writers therefore became dominated by a privileged minority, while a small number eked out a living in the middle range and a growing population of hacks sank into a milieu that, as already explained, can be described as "Grub Street." The French expression "Rousseau du ruisseau" (Rousseaus of the gutter) also suits many of them. In fact, according to Mercier, "sans-culotte" first referred to indigent writers and originated from the scorn heaped on an obscure author, "Gilbert le sans-culotte"—that is, Nicolas Gilbert—who died in 1780 and was so poor that he could not afford decent clothing. "Rich people adopted that expression to deride all authors who were not dressed elegantly," Mercier explained.[18]

A Collective Profile

Having reached some workable estimates of the literary population, we should be able to study its composition. The figure below shows the age distribution of the writers from 1757, 1769, and 1784 whose birth dates can be determined.

They form a minority—48, 36, and 30 percent respectively—of all the authors in the three main editions of *La France littéraire*, but their numbers are sizeable enough to suggest a general pattern. Did the bulk of the literary population come from the young? One might think so, judging from the

AGE OF AUTHORS

IN 1757

IN 1769

IN 1784

AUTHORS

YEARS

Laboratoire de Graphique E.H.E.S.S

No. identified: 565 (48% of total of 1187)
Mean age: 51
Median age: 50

No. identified: 845 (36% of total of 2367)
Mean age: 52
Median age: 51

No. identified: 765 (27% of total of 2819)
Mean age: 53
Median age: 53

Age of known writers, 1757–1784.

literary motif of the lad who abandons a promising career to give vent to his penchant for verse. It was a standard theme, popularized by works like *Le Pauvre Diable*, which Voltaire said he had written "to divert from the career of letters a young man without a fortune, who takes his rage for composing bad verse as a sign of genius. The number of those ruined by this unfortunate passion is prodigious. They make themselves incapable of doing any useful work. . . . They live from rhymes and hopes, and die in destitution."[19] Yet the bar graphs include more writers in their sixties and seventies than in their twenties and thirties, and they indicate an average age of just over fifty in all three groups.

It would be misleading, however, to conclude that the Republic of Letters was not swamped with an influx of young writers as Voltaire believed, because many of the authors in *La France littéraire* had merely produced a volume of essays or verse while pursuing nonliterary careers. Their publications often occurred only in their early twenties, yet they would appear in *La France littéraire* for the rest of their lives, because the editors of the book did not limit its coverage to currently active authors. The graphs should not be taken as evidence of aging within the literary population as a whole, nor do they bear out the opposite thesis—namely, that literature attracted an ever-increasing number of young people. That thesis seems likely, but it cannot be supported by quantitative evidence.

The geographical origins of the authors are shown on the map, which derives from the edition of 1784. (Maps drawn up from the other two editions are virtually the same, so are not reproduced here.) They fall into a pattern familiar to many students of French history. Most writers were born

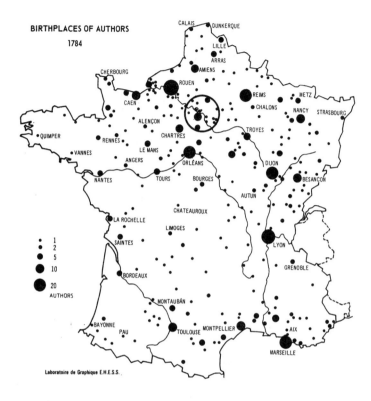

BIRTHPLACES OF AUTHORS
1784

1
2
5
10
20
AUTHORS

Laboratoire de Graphique E.H.E.S.S.

Map of birthplaces of authors, 1784. Number identified: 860, or 31 percent of a total of 2819. Number born in Paris: 170, or 20 percent of the identified.

above the "Maggiolo line" that runs from Saint Malo on the northern coast of Brittany to Geneva, separating the literate North from the relatively unlettered South-Southwest.[20] The northeastern quarter of the kingdom was a particularly fertile source of authors, while Brittany, western Languedoc, and the Massif Central were relatively barren. A large proportion of authors came from cities, particularly Paris and the Paris Basin, and the cities tended to be cultural and administrative centers—the homes of *parlements* and academies—rather than hubs of manufacturing and commerce. Lille (population, 61,467; four authors) and Nantes (population, 77,266; four authors) contributed much less to the total of birthplaces than did Besançon (population, 28,721; eleven authors) and Dijon (population 22,026; twenty authors). Paris (population of about 700,000 in 1789), with its academies, salons, cafés, theaters, and publishing houses, stood out as the center of literary life. *La France littéraire* did not provide information about the current residences of the authors, but other sources indicate that the great majority of them lived in Paris.[21] The map reinforces the view that Paris functioned as a magnet, attracting talent from everywhere in the kingdom. As one writer put it, "Hors de Paris il n'est point de salut" (Outside Paris there is no salvation).[22]

Authors, like everyone else, had a *qualité* or social identity: they might be gentlemen or ladies, clergymen or commoners, members of a profession or artisans; but they fit into the social order in an identifiable way. The nature of the fit might vary, however, according to overlapping or contradictory criteria. *Qualité* could depend upon birth, ownership of an office, the conferring of holy orders, the exercise of a profession, or the means of making a living. No single set of categories will do justice to the complexity of French society under the ancien régime. Nevertheless, one can sort the authors out by estate—clergy, nobility, commoners—and by occupation, as in table 2.2. The socio-occupational position of more than half the authors in each estate can be determined, so the numbers provide a profile of the literary population as a whole. Table 2.3 shows that the privileged orders occupied a disproportionately large place within that population.

Table 2.2. Authors by estate and occupation, 1757–1784.

	1757		1769		1784	
	Number	Percent	Number	Percent	Number	Percent
Upper Clergy, secular	7	1	15	1	13	1
Upper Clergy, regular	4	0	1	0	1	0
Lower Clergy, secular	120	14	194	12	196	13
Lower Clergy, regular	151	17	168	11	91	6
Titled nobility, no office	9	1	21	1	50	3
Officer, upper administration	8	1	20	1	17	1
Officer, military	38	4	85	5	109	7
Officer, sovereign courts	17	2	64	4	42	3
Officer, high finance	8	1	23	1	1	0
Officer, lower courts	6	1	17	1	20	1
Lower administration	42	5	63	4	51	3
Lawyer, Attorney	67	8	169	11	162	11

	1757		1769		1784	
	Number	Percent	Number	Percent	Number	Percent
Law Personnel	2	0	3	0	3	0
Doctor, Surgeon	106	12	231	15	244	16
Apothecary	1	0	13	1	13	1
Engineer/ Architect	17	2	30	2	35	2
Rentier	3	0	2	0	0	0
Lower Finance	4	0	5	0	6	0
Merchant	2	0	9	1	14	1
Manufacturer	1	0	2	0	0	0
Bookseller, Master Printer	5	1	26	2	25	2
Intellectual Trades	198	23	309	20	295	20
Professor	(93	11	165	10	167	11)
Private Teacher	(26	3	44	3	38	3)
Journalist	(9	1	0	0	5	0)
Librarian	(7	1	19	1	23	2)
Interpreter, Translator	(5	1	8	1	12	1)
Secretary	(15	2	15	1	12	1)
Scribe	(2	0	8	1	8	1)
Sinecure	(26	3	15	1	14	1)
Actor, Theater personnel	(8	1	15	1	21	1)
Musician	(7	1	11	1	4	0)

(*continued*)

Table 2.2. Authors by estate and occupation, 1757–1784. (*continued*)

	1757		1769		1784	
	Number	Percent	Number	Percent	Number	Percent
Protestant Clergy	18	2	7	0	8	1
Student	0	0	1	0	1	0
Employee	4	0	8	1	1	0
Shopkeeper	1	0	1	0	4	0
Artisan	8	1	17	1	15	1
Servant	1	0	1	0	0	0
Women, no profession	14	2	42	3	49	3
Other	6	1	30	2	29	2
	868	99	1577	100	1393	98
Unidentified	319		790		1426	
Total	1187		2367		2819	

Table 2.3. Socio-occupational position of authors, 1757–1784.

	1757	1769	1784
Clergy	32%	24%	20%
Nobility	9	12	14
Third Estate	55	59	59
Unidentified	4	5	7

On the eve of the Revolution, a third of the authors belonged to the clergy or nobility, yet those two estates accounted for less than 5 percent of the population. The percentage of clerical authors dropped significantly during the second half of the century, a symptom of the secularization that many historians have detected in the last years of the ancien régime, while the number of noble writers increased somewhat. They particularly flourished in the officer corps of the army, as exemplified by Joseph-Marie Servan de Gerbey, author of *Le Soldat citoyen* (1780). The writer-soldier had eclipsed the writer-prelate—but not ordinary curates, who continued to publish devotional tracts, and independent abbés, who sometimes joined the ranks of the philosophes, as in the case of Gabriel Bonnet de Mably and Guillaume Thomas François Raynal.

The writers from the Third Estate included a large proportion of professional men—engineers, architects, lawyers, and especially doctors. Most of them were provincial savants who treated writing as a secondary occupation and wrote about subjects related to their professions. Professionalism often went hand in hand with a commitment to scientific research and the Enlightenment, as in the case of Dr. Joseph Ignace Guillotin, the champion (not the inventor) of the guillotine, who was one of the Parisian radicals elected to the Estates General in 1789.

By contrast, the industrial and commercial bourgeoisie played little part in the Republic of Letters. *La France littéraire* of 1784 included only fourteen merchants and not a single manufacturer, aside from printers and booksellers. The occupational group that stood out above all the others belonged to what may be called, for lack of a better term, the intellectual trades. Most of the authors in this subcategory were teachers, and most of the teachers were connected with universities—a rather surprising fact in view of the supposed decadence of university life in the eighteenth century. But, for many writers, teaching took the form of part-time employment as a schoolmaster or a tutor in a genteel household. Hack work could also be found in printing shops, libraries, theaters, journals, and scriveners' stalls. The fortunate few found patrons or protectors, who intervened to provide pensions and sinecures. To the writer who lacked an outside income—from an inherited estate, *rentes* (annuities), a benefice, an army commission, an office, or a professional practice—survival depended upon cobbling together odd jobs.

Only a few dozen authors lived by their pens. As mentioned, Mercier estimated their number as thirty in 1778—1 percent of those who appeared in *La France littéraire*. Many of the 99 percent left no trace of their existence aside from their name and the title of a book or two. They had no professional identification, for they had become persons without quality, *gens sans état*. They composed the bulk of Grub Street's population, which did not fit into conventional categories of employment and therefore cannot be calculated. It certainly was large and growing larger, hidden in the increasing number of unidentified writers from *La France littéraire*: 319 in 1757, 790 in 1769, and 1,326 in 1784.

A few writers (Nicolas Restif de la Bretonne is the most famous) belonged to the working classes, but very few—no peasants, no unskilled laborers, and only a handful of artisans and shopkeepers, less than 1 percent of those identified. That working people not only read but also wrote (mainly manuscript journals and letters) is clear from the autobiography of the Parisian glazier Jacques-Louis Ménétra.[23] But they rarely published their writing and so did not win much of a place in *La France littéraire*.

What was the place of women? Du Tertre listed six of them in a separate section of the original *Almanach des beaux arts* entitled "Dames littéraires." It was dropped in later editions, but La Porte paid great attention to women writers. He published a five-volume *Histoire littéraire des femmes françaises* in 1769, just when he completed his most ambitious version of *La France littéraire*. In this version he mixed women with men according to the order of the alphabet, but he had difficulty in placing them professionally. Only a few, like Marie-Jeanne Riccoboni, an actress who churned out bestselling novels, had a distinguishable occupation. The majority wrote as ladies within wealthy bourgeois or aristocratic households. And there weren't many: only fifty-one in 1784, or 3 percent of the total identified.

The quantitative evidence adds up to an unsurprising conclusion: writers belonged for the most part to the traditional elite of the ancien régime. They included a great many members of the privileged orders, an equal number from the professional bourgeoisie, and a large contingent from the intellectual trades. Their share of manufacturers, workers, and women was disproportionately small. And they lacked writers of the modern variety—the kind who lived by their pens as independent intellectuals. Of course, an intelligentsia of sorts was already forming: it grew up around Voltaire, Diderot, and the other philosophes. But it did not develop a clear social identity and a firm economic base. At one end, the intelligentsia extended to the refined world of the salons. At the other, it shaded off into Grub Street, the marginal element in the Republic of Letters, which lay outside the bounds of polite society.

CONTEMPORARY VIEWS

T HERE IS SOMETHING unreal about the graphs, maps, and socio-occupational tables that can be used to take the measure of the literary population in the eighteenth century. Nothing could be further from the writers' sense of their experience. Yet they lived through the phenomena that we cut apart and rearrange according to the conventions of our own mode of analysis. What would those phenomena look like if translated back into terms used by the writers themselves? Fortunately, eighteenth-century authors produced an enormous literature about authorship.[1] Much of it merely vented squabbles and lamentations of a parochial sort, but some can be read as a commentary on what contemporaries construed as the facts of literary life. Two such works stand out: *Le Petit Almanach de nos grands hommes* (1788) by Antoine Rivarol and *Les Gens de lettres* (1787) by P.-F.-N. Fabre d'Egalantine.[2]

Satire

At first glance, Rivarol's almanac looks like a sequel to La Porte's *France littéraire*. It presents itself as a survey of all the authors in France, or at least all the poets, for Rivarol generally restricted his coverage to belles lettres and promised to provide entries on the most obscure authors of the least memorable madrigals. The names file by in alphabetical order, accompanied by references to the *Almanach des muses*, the *Étrennes de Polymnie*, the *Almanach des grâces*, the *Étrennes d'Apollon*, and a dozen other publications where unknown writers unloaded epigrams, couplets, *bouts rimés, pièces fugitives*, and anything else that might catch the public's eye. The poems are so trivial and the poets so obscure that one soon realizes the "almanach" is a joke, an elaborate satire about literary life at a time when the supply of *sensiblerie* had far exceeded the demand. By combing through all the ephemera of his day, Rivarol produced a stupendous roll call of mediocrities. He turned the literary world upside down, burying the most famous writers in silence and exposing the smallest fry to the grossest praise. Thus

COQUART (M.). His couplets are the only ones in fashion.
CONTANT D'ORVILLE (M.). He is the hope of the madrigal.
PERROT (M.). Master poet and tailor in Paris. He favors tragedies, and here are two lines by him that are very well known and very pathetic:

Hélas, hélas hélas et quatre fois hélas,
Il lui coupa le cou d'un coup de coutelas.

Alas, alas, alas, and four times alas,
He cut off his neck with a blow of a cutlass.[3]

Rivarol's withering gaze took in the entire population of fifth-rate scribblers and exposed all their maneuvers to escape from obscurity. They submitted poems to all the literary reviews. They competed in all the essay contests of the provincial academies. And if no one would print their work, they circulated it in cafés and declaimed it in literary clubs like the Musée de Paris, which was open to everyone and contained so many aspiring men of letters that the most unpublished of them was sure to find an audience. Rivarol pretended to rescue these undiscovered geniuses from oblivion by printing their names and overwhelming them with praise. Somehow, however, the praise always undid itself, thanks to a few well-placed absurdities. Thus the non sequitur followed by an impossible metaphor in the notice on J.-A. Rigoley de Juvigny: "A writer perfectly unknown, thanks to his eloquence, poetry, philosophy, and erudition; to such an extent has envy been on the look-out for this great man! We hope to make our century blush with shame for having left in obscurity the person who enlightened it." A little overstatement sufficed to dispatch Pons de Verdun: "A literary Hercules. One knows that he did not fear to sign about ten thousand epigrams and tales in verse and to send them to all the almanacs and journals." And overpraise undercut everyone associated with the Musée. Rivarol dedicated his almanac to J.-F. Cailhava de l'Estendoux, "President of the Great Musée of Paris," whom he described as marching heroically "at the head of five or six hundred poets. Our almanac will be for them the Book of Life, because it will provide the most unknown man with a diploma of immortality. There are, it is said, well known paths for arriving at the Académie, but none are known for escaping from the Musée."

The burlesque almanac conveyed a kind of satirical sociology; and the satire hit home, because it cut deep into literary life—life as it was actually lived by most French writers, not in a rarefied Republic of Letters but in garrets, cafés, and the columns of third-rate reviews. Rivarol had a sharp eye for such settings, because he knew his way around the literary circles of Paris.[4] Instead of inventing his material, he picked it up from his contacts and by reading journals. To be sure, he made his victims look so absurd that one may suspect him of inventing everything in their mock biographical notices, including their existence. But Rivarol usually documented his assertions, and they can be confirmed by following up his references. Thus a typical short notice: "DUPRAY (M.). Has proved his existence in the *Almanach des muses*." Although Dupray cannot be found in any modern bibliography, he appears, exactly as Rivarol indicated, in the *Almanach des muses* (Paris, 1782), pp. 61–62. Some references strain credulity, as in Rivarol's pairing of two provincial versifiers, M. Briquet and M. Braquet. But far from being characters invented to illustrate the bric-a-brac of literature, the two can be found, just as Rivarol noted, in the *Muses provinciales* of 1788, Briquet as the author of an "Ode tirée du Pseaume 129," Braquet as the author of an allegory.[5] Every author in *Le Petit Almanach*, no matter how laughable, seems to have actually existed. In fact, Rivarol did his research so thoroughly that it is relevant to the question of literary demography. He identified 672 poets—a staggering number, if one considers that *La France littéraire* listed only 2,819 writers of all varieties in 1784. In quantitative terms along, *Le Petit Almanach* demonstrated the severity of the population problem in literature.

Rivarol's rhetoric, for all its tendentiousness, shows how that problem entered into contemporary discourse about literature. In a facetious preface, Rivarol claimed that his book originated from a parlor game improvised by two Parisian wits. Tired of discussing the great authors of the past, they took up "the small literature" of the present. One named an obscure writer and challenged the other to identify him. After meeting the challenge, the other riposted with an equally unknown name. The competition warmed as the names flew back and forth. It was the world's first trivia contest. "Mérard de Saint-Just," called out the first wit. "Joli de Plancy," answered the second. "Lourdet de Santerre," came the reply; and "Regnault de Beaucaron," the counterattack. It was "Briquet" here and "Braquet" there; "Guinguenet," "Moutonnet," "Fricot," "Pistolet," "Mitraille," "Cathala-Cotire"—an "army of Lilliputians" on either side with salvoes of titles so unfamiliar that the onlookers finally protested. The contestants had to be making it up. Certainly not, they retorted indignantly. There really was a writer named Levrier de Champrion and another known as Delormel de la Rotière. They could prove it, given an adequate supply of *almanachs* and *étrennes*. So the parlor game turned into a research project, and the result was *Le Petit Almanach de nos grands hommes*.

At this point, Rivarol, who claimed to write as a witness to the contest, adopted a philosophic view of his subject and changed metaphors:

> For me, a benevolent auditor, struck by the rich nomenclature of so many unknown writers, I could not prevent myself from an observation that I shared with my neighbors. . . .

> "Is it not," I said to them "very strange and very humiliating for the human species this mania of historians to cite only a dozen at most of the great writers? . . . If I wrote a work of natural history, do you think I would name only elephants, rhinoceroses, and whales? Certainly not, Messieurs, I would descend with pleasure from those imposing colossi to the smallest animalcules, and you would sense your admiration for nature grow and become more tender when I arrived at the innumerable crowd of families, of tribes, of nations, of republics and empires hidden beneath a leaf of grass."

The phrasing played on the public's passion for herborizing and natural history, but it also reduced the writers to the level of insects. Voltaire had hammered away at this theme a generation earlier. In *Le Pauvre Diable*, he had treated "low literature" as a population problem: "Egypt of old had fewer locusts."[6] Rivarol picked up the theme where Voltaire had left it. In fact, he remarked facetiously that Voltaire would have used *Le Petit Almanach* as a reference work, had it been available while he was writing *Le Pauvre Diable*.

But in Rivarol's version, the picture of low literature as an underworld of insects looked more menacing. Although the creatures swarming in obscurity might appear ridiculous, they could scratch and sting. Thus Jean-Louis Carra: "After having written fifteen or sixteen volumes of physics on the atom, the apatom, and the exatom, which everyone knows by heart, he did not disdain to fall upon M. de Calonne. Armed with all the thunderbolts of eloquence, he gave the final blow to the dying lion." Rivarol was referring to Carra's *M. de Calonne tout entier*, a crucial pamphlet in the barrage of radical protest that helped drive the finance minister Charles-Alexandre de Calonne from the government and finally from France during the crisis surrounding the Assembly of Notables in 1787. *Le Petit Almanach* appeared a year later. In it the first rumblings of the Revolution can already be heard.

Yet Rivarol did not treat literature as a political phenomenon or foresee the collapse of the ancien régime, and there was nothing prophetic about the appearance of future Jacobins in his catalog of the lower literati. Their names stand out, nonetheless, at least to the postrevolutionary reader: Fabre d'Églantine, Collot d'Herbois, Desmoulins, Fréron, Manuel, Mercier, Gorsas. Rivarol could have added more. In fact he did so in a sequel to his almanac, *Le Petit Dictionnaire de nos grands hommes de la Révolution* (1790), which included Emmanuel-Joseph Sieyès, Jacques-Pierre Brissot, Georges Jacques Danton, Jean-Paul Marat, Dominique Joseph Garat, Jerome Pétion, and "Roberspierre," whom Rivarol hailed as the author of a madrigal "which was the despair of M. de Voltaire in his old age."[7] By this time, however, literature had become politicized. Rivarol did not read politics into literature before 1789; and his reading of it should not be taken as evidence that life at the bottom of the literary world led inevitably to Jacobinism, because most of his poor poets disappeared forever into the obscurity from which he pretended to rescue them. *Le Petit Almanach* merely indicates the vastness of that obscurity—its cruelty, too, and its importance as an element in the prerevolutionary understanding of literature.

Sentiment

For a contrasting view, one that would feed into revolutionary rather than counterrevolutionary ideology, we should turn to *Les Gens de lettres* by Fabre d'Églantine. Fabre's play, a five-act *drame bourgeois* in rhyming couplets, was performed at the Comédie Italienne on September 21, 1787. According to a review in the *Correspondance littéraire*, the audience hooted it off the stage: "It was impossible for us to follow the plot of this play because of the booing and whistling that never ceased from the pit during its first and last performance." The reviewer did not dispute the public's judgment: "It is difficult to imagine a play whose plot is colder and more badly woven, and its style did not nearly compensate for the lack of intrigue and action." The author could be identified vaguely as an "actor from the provinces who was not known by any other production," but he was hard to place in the flood of provincial writers who came to seek their fortune in Paris.[8] Fabre's actual place, before he joined the front ranks of the revolutionaries, was among the unknown authors of *Le Petit Almanach*. Rivarol had skewered him with sardonic compliments:

> FABRE D'ÉGLANTINE (M.). The success of his plays in the Comédie française and the Comédie italienne is equaled by the prodigious fortune of his couplets, which are the charm of polite society.

Fabre fit perfectly into the world that Rivarol satirized. As already mentioned, he had sought his fortune in provincial theaters for fifteen years, acting and writing skits. In 1787 he settled into some furnished rooms in Paris and began campaigning to get his work performed on the stages of the capital. A job as secretary to the marquis of Ximenès procured some contacts, if not much income. And in the autumn, the Comédie Italienne agreed to put on *Les Gens de lettres*, whose subtitle sounded like a description of Fabre's own situation: *Le poète provincial à Paris*.[9]

The play did not leave much of a mark on French literature—apparently it has never been performed since its disastrous first night, and it was not published until 1827, thirty-three years after Fabre's death—but it shows how the world looked to one of Rivarol's little great men. The hero, an undiscovered genius from the provinces named Clar, tries to write his way out of a garret in a rooming house. He has to cope with an imposing cast of villains: Mme Robur, his penny-pinching landlady who spies for the police; Quotidien, a journalist who cannot distinguish between book reviewing and bribery; Musophage, a publisher who treats poetry as finance and poets as scum; Lacrimant, a dramatist who will not tolerate any kind of writing other than his own; the count of Espérie, an aristocratic influence peddler; and a coterie of beaux esprits led by Fastidor, a fashionable fop who pretends to be consumed by *sensibilité* but is actually devoured by ambition and partisanship.

How is a poor provincial lad to negotiate through such hostile territory? In his innocence, Clar remains at his desk, composing one masterpiece after another. His devoted servant, Richard, keeps them both alive by hiring himself out to clean floors in the rooming house. At one point, Clar tries to raise some money by offering a manuscript to Musophage, but instead of providing relief, the proposal gives the publisher an opportunity to parade his importance and to dictate humiliating terms:

Voici le compte clair qu'avec vous je veux suivre:
Par un écrit formel et dûment cimenté,
Vous allez me céder avec perpétuité

> L'ouvrage dont s'agit, avec liberté pleine
> De le trancher, couper, tailler, rogner, sans gêne.

> Here is the clear agreement that I want to settle with you:
> By a formal and duly fixed contract,
> You will cede to me the perpetual rights
> To the given work, with full liberty
> To slit, cut, slice, and trim it with no restraint.[10]

In return, Clar is to receive the miserable sum of two louis, not in cash but in copies of the book, which he then may peddle to booksellers—provided that he keep out of the best-known bookstores of the Latin Quarter and the lesser shops of the Palais-Royal and the Louvre and limit himself to the quais and the Luxembourg Gardens.

This harangue, which goes on for seventy lines of unpoetic detail about practices in the publishing industry, demonstrates an axiom that Fabre took for granted: a writer could not live by his pen. A second basic fact is made clear at the beginning of the play, when a character observes:

> Qu'il tombe ici des poètes des nues
> Et qu'autant vaut compter les pavés dans les rues.[11]

> That poets are raining down here from the sky,
> And are as numerous as cobblestones in the street.

The only escape from the underpaid and overpopulated conditions of authorship lay through protection—a third fundamental fact, which Fabre dramatized in the central scene of the play. Hoping to find some support for his master, Clar's servant secretly slips one of his poems into a gathering of literati. They immediately recognize its worth;

but fearing a rival or a potential ally of an enemy clique, they condemn Clar's work and conspire to keep it unknown. Protection is mediated through cabals of established writers, who dominate the academies, salons, and journals—fact four. For a moment in a following scene, it looks as though Clar may overcome all these obstacles, because a sympathetic character announces that he knows a count, who knows a marquis, who knows a minister. A secretarial job is rumored to be dangling at the end of this line of influence. Clar's first thought when he began to go under was for just such a sinecure:

> Il demande, il espère
> Auprès d'un grand seigneur l'emploi de secrétaire.[12]

> He asks for, he hopes for
> The job of a secretary to a great nobleman

But he lacks the connections necessary to make it through this opening in the wall of privileges, and it closes, leaving him stranded outside the respectable world of letters.

Every turn of the plot has demonstrated that the facts of literary life are stacked against underprivileged, unprotected genius. How then does Clar find a way through to the denouement? By a deus ex machina in the person of Damis, the secondary hero of the play. Damis is pure provincial, all virtue, and rich. Having sampled literary life in Paris, he is about to return in disgust to his country estate when he discovers Clar. He does not hesitate a moment:

> Prenez ces mille écus . . .
> Apprenez qu'un bienfait ne fit jamais de honte.
> Prenez ces trois billets de la Caisse d'escompte.[13]

> Take these thousand écus . . .
> Know that beneficence never causes shame.
> Take these three bills of exchange on the Caisse d'escompte.

In classical drama, alexandrines did not end with words like Caisse d'escompte. Fabre called cash *cash*. He celebrated the link between money and poetry, but he never suggested that a writer could support himself on the literary marketplace. For Clar as for every other successful author, salvation comes from patronage. Yet far from being well connected in court, his patron is a bourgeois gentleman. Not a representative of entrepreneurial capitalism, however, because Damis has merely inherited a fortune worth thirty thousand livres a year from an aunt who died in India. Instead of adding a note of realism to the plot, he appears as a sort of fairy godfather and whisks Clar off to the provinces, where they will write masterpieces together happily ever after. The play contains some strong social criticism, but in the end it turns into an escapist fantasy of a writer trapped in Grub Street.

Of course, fantasies can be revealing as a source of social history, and Fabre's imagination did not fly so high above his surroundings as to make them unrecognizable. On the contrary, his critics accused him of producing a caricature of the literary world. They saw real figures everywhere in his cast of characters.[14] And whether or not their "keys" identified the persons correctly, it is clear that the dramatis personae embodied everything that Fabre found hateful in literature as a social system—the exclusiveness, the string-pulling, the dominance of a few established writers and their aristocratic protectors in "the party of tyrants."[15]

Fabre drew this conclusion from his own experience, but it also has a literary source: the works of Jean-Jacques Rousseau.[16] Rousseau's influence stands out on every page of Fabre's text. Fabre even cites him as the ideal type of a writer, a pure genius who maintained his purity by withdrawing to a garret and copying music instead of compromising with the literary system.[17] Clar embodied that ideal, which is accompanied throughout the play by Rousseauistic motifs—the virtue of country life as opposed to the corruption of the city, the decency of the common people in contrast to the decadence of the aristocracy, and catch words such as "pity," "virtue," and "nature."[18] The chief villain of the play is a count who operates as a confidence man, and the noblest character is the humblest, Clar's servant Richard, who inspires a soliloquy by Damis on social injustice and natural equality:

> Et puis, écoutez bien la voix du philosophe.
> Nous naissons tous pareils et d'une même étoffe.[19]

> And then, listen well to the voice of the philosopher.
> We are all born similarly from the same stuff.

Fabre's indictment of the literary world reads like an attack on the entire social order. In sentiment and style, it is virtually Jacobin, five years before full-blown Jacobinism was conceivable.

Le Petit Almanach de nos grands hommes and *Les Gens de lettres* can serve as glosses on the statistics presented earlier. Rivarol heaped derision on the struggle for survival of obscure authors; Fabre elevated it into a moralistic drama. They construed the same subject in opposite ways—hence the importance of comparing them, for we may calculate the vital statistics of literary life in a manner that robs them of their vitality. We need to know what the underlying conditions of literature meant to the writers who experienced them. Rivarol and Fabre did not disagree about those conditions, but they interpreted them differently by drawing on different literary genres. One presented the world of letters in the form of a burlesque almanac, the other as a *drame bourgeois*. One saw it from the viewpoint of Voltaire, the other from that of Rousseau. Their rhetoric expressed an ideological divide, and the division widened after the outbreak of the Revolution, when Rivarol and Fabre enlisted in opposed camps. Yet we should resist the temptation to read too much of a revolutionary or counterrevolutionary disposition into their writings before 1789. Indeed, I would run the argument in the opposite direction: Rivarol and Fabre read themes from their prerevolutionary writings into the Revolution, which drew writers into a war of words fired off from positions staked out under the ancien régime.

Sequels

Rivarol and Fabre followed up their prerevolutionary manifestos with sequels, which show how literature fed into the Revolution's transformation of the world. Rivarol's *Petit Dictionnaire des grands hommes de la Révolution* (1790) used the same formula as his *Petit Almanach de nos grands hommes*: biographical notices arranged alphabetically and crammed with such extravagant language as to make its victims look ridiculous. But he shifted to politics, and as a partisan of the Right, he pilloried leaders of the Left. He opposed values from the ancien régime—honor, loyalty to the king, respect for birth, and refinement in taste—to what he derided as a new barbarism composed of violence, vulgarity, and careerism among revolutionaries who exploited the passions of the mob. Yet this theme, so common to counterrevolutionary propaganda, had a curiously belletristic character. The strongest article in Rivarol's indictment of the National Assembly was aesthetic:

> It is also from this august assembly that we have seen the blossoming of geniuses, which, without it, would still be the boring rejects of society. What miracles patriotism offers! The heaviest dolts of literature have proven to be the profoundest members of the assembly; the most notorious ignoramuses of French youth have not seemed embarrassed, nor out of place in the Parisian tribune: in short, the enemies of the language have suddenly become the defenders of the nation.[20]

The "great men" of the Revolution sinned in the same way as their predecessors from the ancien régime; they sinned against language.

Rivarol poured most of his scorn on radical orators and journalists: Fabre, Mirabeau, Marat, Brissot, Desmoulins, Danton, Carra, Garat, Gorsas, Pétion, Manuel, Elysée Loustalot, Louis-Marie Prudhomme, and Robespierre (always misspelled, intentionally, as "Roberspierre"). He objected more vehemently to their use of words than to their stance on political issues, although he took such a literary view of politics that he hardly distinguished form from substance. Thus, his article on Desmoulins:

It is in the street that M. Desmoulins has established himself with his eloquence, and he has the passersby as admirers. With three learned words—nation, lamppost,[21] and aristocrat—he has been able to put himself within the understanding of the honest butcher boy, the modest fisherwoman, and all those new readers produced by the revolution. It is such pens that are necessary to lead the common people and to accustom them to having ideas.[22]

Rivarol condemned Prudhomme's *Révolutions de Paris* for fomenting sedition with the same vulgarity: "For a simple newspaper to have such a great effect, it's necessary for its style to express its purpose and for it to become the charm of the most barbarous reader."

It hardly seems surprising that the author of the celebrated essay *De l'Universalité de la langue française* (1784) should have shown a concern for language. But Rivarol now defended aesthetic standards as if they were social distinctions. He identified the champions of the people with the lower ranks of writers and condemned their rise to power as a rebellion against everyone and everything of eminence in literature. The freeing of the press had touched off a social revolution within the world of letters. "What a noble source of abundance the liberty of the press has given us! It has merely ruined talent and good taste—that is, a few individuals who humiliated a million poor writers. The equality of the mind has thus become one of the greatest operations of the National Assembly."[23] Rivarol took consolation from the thought that the Revolution found no supporters in respectable literary circles and the Académie française, except for a few aberrations like Jean-Sylvain Bailly, an academician who was misled by "the noble simplicity of his character."[24] The rabble drew its rousers from inferior scribblers, making the Revolution look like an extension of the population pressure under the ancien régime.

Of course, Rivarol recognized that the Revolution involved a great deal more than literature. He used the aesthetic argument tendentiously as a way to satirize its leaders, and he extended the satire to make the Revolution appear as the work of failures from every milieu: "It is by a perfect accord between the scum of the court and of fortune that we have arrived at the general misery that alone attests to our equality."[25] The old almanac provided a "model," as he put it, for his account of revolutionary politics.[26] From one book to another, the message remained the same: France was being overwhelmed with mediocrity. The "great men" of the Revolution succeeded the "great men" of the old literary regime, dooming France to disaster.

In February 1790, at about the same time that Rivarol published the sequel to his *Petit Almanach*, the Théâtre français put on a new play by Fabre, *Le Philinte de Molière*. Fabre presented it as a sequel to Molière's *Le Misanthrope*, although it also can be read as a continuation of *Les Gens de lettres*, because it took up where his earlier play had left off. Disgusted with the hypocritical conventions in Paris, Damis had withdrawn to his country estate at the end of *Les Gens de lettres*, exactly as Alceste had done in the last act of *Le Misanthrope*. Fabre brought him back to Paris reincarnated as Alceste in *Le Philinte de Molière*. He then added other characters from Molière's play and extended the plot through a new set of intrigues.

Philinte has married Eliante, bought a title, and given himself over to the pleasures of high society when Alceste arrives, declaiming as usual against hypocrisy and immorality. Philinte replies with a defense of the ways of the world, but he soon falls victim to them, because a swindler and a corrupt attorney conspire to strip him of his wealth by means of a fraudulent bill of exchange. Alceste parries their blow to his friend by offering to sacrifice his own fortune. Then he finds an honest lawyer—a poor but virtuous, fearless, dedicated defender of the oppressed—and together they confound the villains. The real villain of the play, however, turns out to be Philinte. He cares for nothing but his self-interest, and he will stop at nothing, from peddling influence to abandoning Alceste, in order to promote it. In the denouement, therefore, he is the one confounded. After rescuing him, Alceste reads him a lecture on the importance of virtue and retires once again to the simple life in the country, accompanied by the lawyer.

Les Gens de lettres had ended in the same way. In fact, it, too, can be read as a sentimentalized rewriting of Molière. When Henri Meister reviewed it in the *Correspondance littéraire*, he treated it as a failed attempt to produce a modern version of *Les Femmes savantes*. By following Molière, Meister observed, Fabre had seized on a promising subject, the pretensions of unknown and unpublished *littérateurs*. But he had spoiled it by treating the writers—that is, Clar and Damis—as heroes instead of as clowns. Molière would have ridiculed the entire population of obscure scribblers who had assumed the title of *gens de lettres*, "a term that inspires respectability which they use to give themselves a rank, a standing in society."[27] A few months later, in *Le Petit*

Almanach de nos grands hommes, Rivarol published precisely the satire that Meister had called for, and Meister applauded him.[28] But Fabre avoided anything that suggested comedy. When he rewrote Molière, he turned *Le Misanthrope* upside down. The hero (or, arguably, the most appealing character, Philinte) became the villain, and the villain (or at least the principal target of Molière's satire, Alceste) became the hero. Favre emptied the play of humor and filled it with moralistic declamations. Nothing could have been further from the spirit of the original.

Yet Fabre kept to the same cast of characters and the same setting. In the midst of the Revolution, while the Bastille was being dismantled, feudalism abolished, and a new civil order constructed from the ruins of the old, he produced a period piece, completely devoid of political commentary. Aside from a few veiled allusions to current events—an irreverent remark about the aristocracy here, an oblique reference to the rights of man there—he might have been writing in another world, the France of Louis XIV.[29] Why? Why this obsession with a literary theme more than a hundred years old? Fabre could have chosen a more obviously revolutionary subject—an episode from the Roman republic, perhaps, or something about Americans or Quakers or William Tell. Why did he choose Molière?

The play could not have been out of tune with the times, because the public, already primed to applaud revolutionary theater by the success of M. J. Chénier's *Charles IX*, gave it a warm reception.[30] Even the critics liked it. The most fastidious of them, J.-F. La Harpe, who had scorned *Les Gens de lettres* but had rallied to the Left in 1789, hailed Fabre's work as a triumph of eloquence and of virtue over vice. Camille Desmoulins treated it as a masterpiece. To be sure, Desmoulins could be expected to shower Fabre with praise. They were friends and fellow activists in the radical Cordelier Club. Fabre was then president of the Cordelier District and a mainstay of the club, which included a great many men of letters and lawyers—so many, in fact, that when it moved into the former quarters of the Musée de Paris, rue Dauphine, in 1791, it seemed to be following a script prepared by Rivarol, who, as mentioned, had facetiously dedicated his *Petit Almanach* to the Musée. A discerning eye might even detect something of Danton, the leader of the Cordelier radicals, in the poor but fearless lawyer glorified in Fabre's script. By making a hero of him just as he had celebrated the poor but talented poet in *Les Gens de lettres*, Fabre appealed to an important element in his constituency and in the newly radicalized theater public.

How that public perceived the play can be inferred from Desmoulins's review of it. Desmoulins, who did not normally review plays in his journal, went over its plot and characters in detail, as if it were perfectly natural to be discussing Molière at a time when, as he noted, "even in the theater all eyes turn to the National Assembly, to politics and legislation."[31] He reported that the spectators sitting around him reacted as he did. When one of them objected that Philinte's egoism seemed exaggerated, a dozen others retorted, "That's just the way he is; I've seen him; I know a thousand just like him."[32] They did not see a historical drama so much as a confrontation between virtue and vice.[33] Those abstractions took on a political meaning, because the triumph of virtue was the supreme goal of the Revolution as understood by members of the Cordelier Club. To them (and to many revolutionaries, notably Robespierre), radical politics meant unmasking hypocrisy and exposing egoism. So, Desmoulins could present Fabre's rewriting of Molière as a political act: it advanced the cause of revolution and marked a victory for the Cordeliers, who shared in its success "as a collective triumph."[34]

The notion of politics as a matter of morals was also a theme of literary history. It went back to the ancients, but its immediate source, for Fabre and the entire revolutionary Left, was the writings of Rousseau. In a prologue to the play, Fabre himself took the stage and dramatically drew a copy of Rousseau's *Lettre à M. d'Alembert sur les spectacles* from his pocket. Then he announced,

> C'est à ce livre, à son intention,
> Que je dois mon ouvrage et sa conception;
> Je le dis hautement. Si le méchant m'assiège,
> Qu'il sache que Rousseau lui-même me protège.[35]

> It is to this book, to its intent,
> That I owe my work and its conception;
> I will say it openly. If someone wicked attacks me,
> He should know that Rousseau himself is my protector.

The source could hardly be mistaken, for in his *Lettre à M. d'Alembert* Rousseau had shaken up the Republic of Letters and had broken with his fellow philosophes by an extraordinary tour de force of literary criticism: he reinterpreted *Le Misanthrope* as a moral drama with Alceste in the role of the hero, and he transformed the dramatical question into an arraignment of the ancien régime.

If the genealogy of Fabre's play appears clear, however, its significance seems puzzling, at least to the modern reader. All this interpreting and reinterpreting looks like a game of mirrors: Desmoulins's version of Fabre's version of Rousseau's version of Molière's version of the conflict between inflexible morality and social convention. Why did this literary game matter so much to the French revolutionaries? Given the press of other business—the need to dismantle one world and to build another—why did they play it at all?

Cultural Revolution

The answer to this puzzle goes back to a fundamental task of the French Revolution and a basic tension within "literary France."

To the people in the midst of it, the French Revolution tore apart a familiar world and left them with the need to make sense of a new order that was confusedly coming into being. That task fell to the intellectuals—that is, to the people who had a way with words and who had played with words for years among the ranks of the three thousand writers under what, in retrospect, appeared as an ancien régime. Fabre, for instance, did not merely rework *Le Misanthrope*; he helped to reorder time by producing a nomenclature for the new, rational, natural, revolutionary calendar. To rewrite Molière and to redesign time belonged to the same endeavor, the social reconstruction of reality.

One cannot remake reality ex nihilo. The intellectuals fell back on their experience and worked with themes they had inherited from the ancien régime. They opposed

Rousseauistic moralizing to Voltairean satire, and they framed their pronouncements in familiar genres: the *drame bourgeois* vs. the burlesque almanac, the Ciceronian declamation vs. the bon mot. The form was as important as the content, because the radical journalists and orators did not distinguish style from substance. They hated satire the way they hated high society, and they distrusted wit as a sign of an aristocratic disposition.

Their attitudes varied, of course. Some made use of humor: hence the belly laugh of Hébert's *Père Duchesne* and the mockery of Desmoulins's *Vieux Cordelier*. But even these seemed treasonous to Robespierre. When he looked back at the literature of the ancien régime, he saw an alien world of refinement and corruption. Although he acknowledged the importance of the Enlightenment as "the preface to our Revolution," he smashed the bust of Helvétius in the Jacobin Club and vilified the Encyclopedists: "These coryphées [the high priests of the *Encyclopédie* sect] occasionally declaimed against despotism, yet they were pensioned by despots; they produced books against the court, yet they wrote dedications to kings, discourses for courtiers, and madrigals for ladies of the court; they were proud in their books and servile in the antechambers of the great."[36]

"Men of letters" in general seemed suspicious to Robespierre. Having guillotined a heavy proportion of writers among the Girondins, Hébertistes, and Dantonistes, he deplored their role in the Revolution and singled out only one writer from the ancien régime for praise—Jean-Jacques Rousseau:

One man, by the elevation of his soul and by the grandeur of his character, proved worthy of being the tutor of the

human race. [Rousseau] boldly attacked tyranny; he spoke
of the divinity with enthusiasm; his virile and upright eloquence painted the beauties of virtue in strokes of fire; he
defended the consoling tenets that reason gives to fortify
the human heart. The purity of his doctrine, drawn from
nature and from a profound hatred of vice, as well as his
invincible scorn for the intriguing sophists who usurped the
name of philosopher, brought down upon him the hatred
and persecution of his rivals and his false friends.[37]

On October 24, 1793, Fabre presented his project for the
revolutionary calendar to the Convention, which had been
called after the overthrow of the monarchy to produce a
republican constitution. When he listed the patriotic festivals to be celebrated at the end of the year, he put Genius
first and Virtue third. Robespierre objected. Virtue must
come first, he insisted. It was a moral force essential to a
republic, whereas Genius was nothing more than a literary quality, possessed by men like Voltaire: "Voltaire wrote
Brutus; Voltaire was a man of genius, but the hero of the
poem [Brutus] was more worthy than the poet."[38] A few
months later, Robespierre denounced Fabre as an artful
intriguer who used his experience on the stage to cabal and
corrupt citizens "in the theater of the Revolution."[39] When
Robespierre reworked Rousseau's ideas, he took them off
the stage and into the street. He marched them about Paris
in the Festival to the Supreme Being; and he turned them
against Fabre himself, who went to the guillotine as a kind
of Philinte, the essence of corruption in the eyes of the
Incorruptible.

The revolutionaries used Rousseau in different ways at
different times. I do not mean to imply that they spoke with

one voice or that the literary dimension of the Revolution was simple and unanimous. I am arguing, rather, that it belonged to a common task, which arises in all great revolutions, the necessity of remaking reality from the rubble of an old regime. As products of the literary system peculiar to the ancien régime in France, the writers of the Revolution revolutionized through literature. They began in 1789–1790 by capturing the sacred center of the old literary system— the space shaped by Molière—and they ended in 1792–1794 by working it into the core of a new political culture. If I may steal a leaf from Pierre Bourdieu, I think it is helpful to envisage literary France as a "field" of power relations organized around two opposing "poles," the ideological and aesthetic positions embodied by Voltaire and Rousseau. There were also intermediate positions—Diderot's, for example—but the opposition of Voltaire and Rousseau defined the struggle to dominate the "symbolic goods" peculiar to that field— not merely the wealth, status, and power conferred on the most prestigious writers, but the very conception of literature itself.

Consider the way literature figures in the most important works of those two writers. First, Voltaire. His long, complex, and evolving oeuvre can hardly be reduced to a formula, not even "écrasez l'infâme" (crush the infamous thing), but a key word lies at the heart of it: *politesse*. In 1730, Voltaire was overwhelmed by an incident, which haunted him for the rest of his life. The great actress Adrienne Lecouvreur suddenly died after playing the lead in his tragedy *Oedipe*. Voltaire, who may have been her lover, sat by her at her deathbed. She did not receive the last sacraments, because she had not renounced her profession. Actors and actresses were treated as infidels by the Church, and therefore her body could not be buried in sacred ground. It was dumped in a ditch and covered with quicklime to speed its decomposition.

This obscene act obsessed Voltaire right up to the moment of his own death, when he feared that his body would receive the same treatment. It appears in some of his most impassioned poetry, in the *Lettres philosophiques*, and even in *Candide*. In chapter 22, Candide visits Paris and is told the story in all its horror. He then remarks, "That was very impolite."[40] Not what we would expect as a reaction to a barbaric brutality that had set a friend's (or lover's) blood to boil.

The first characteristic Candide noticed among the inhabitants of the utopian society of Eldorado was their "extreme politeness."[41] He marveled at their good manners, elegant clothing, sumptuous housing, exquisite food, sophisticated conversation, refined taste, and superb wit. Those qualities were epitomized by the king of Eldorado, "who received them with all imaginable grace and politely invited them to supper."[42] Utopia is above all a society that is polite and policed ("une société polie" and "policée"), which comes down to the same thing.

The discussion of Voltaire's politics can get snagged on a badly put question ("une question mal posée"). Was he a liberal? A champion of enlightened absolutism? A man of the Left, the Center, or the Right? In fact, Voltaire understood politics according to categories that antedated all those terms and that no longer exist. "There are only three ways of keeping men under control," he wrote, "that of policing them by proposing laws, that of using religion to support those laws, and finally that of slaughtering one part of a nation in order to govern the other part."[43] The three methods really came down to two: politics was a matter of tyranny on one hand, or an "État policé" (reinforced by religion) on the other.

The eighteenth-century notion of "police" could be translated roughly as rational administration. It belonged (conceptually, not etymologically) to a series of interlocking terms—*poli, police, policé, politique*—which extended from culture to politics. For Voltaire, the cultural system of the ancien régime shaded off into a power system, and the code of polite society belonged to the politics of a well-run absolute monarchy.

The interpenetration of culture and politics is the main theme of Voltaire's great treatise, *Le Siècle de Louis XIV*.[44] This was a crucial work for eighteenth-century authors, a book that defined the literary system of the ancien régime and that created literary history in France. In *Le Siècle de Louis XIV* Voltaire argued, in effect, that all history is driven by literary history. Kings, queens, and generals do not count in the long run, although they attract most of the attention of their contemporaries—and actually occupy a large part of Voltaire's narrative. What matters above all is civilization. Therefore, of the four happy ages in the history of mankind, the greatest was the age of Louis XIV, when French literature reached its zenith and the politeness—"la politesse et l'esprit de société"—of the French court set a standard for all of Europe.[45]

By civilization, Voltaire meant something akin to Norbert Elias's "civilizing process." It is the moving force of history, a combination of aesthetic and social elements, manners and mores ("moeurs"), which pushes society toward the ideal of El Dorado, a state in which men are perfectly "poli" and "policé." So, Voltaire understood *politesse* as power, and he saw an essential connection between classical French literature and the absolutism of the French state under Louis XIV. This argument underlies the key episodes of *Le Siècle de Louis XIV*. Louis masters the French language by studying the works of Corneille. He controls the court by staging plays. And he dominates the kingdom by turning the court itself into an exemplary theater. That idea may be a cliché now, but Voltaire (with help from Saint Simon) invented it. He saw power as performance—the acting out of a cultural code. The code spread from Versailles to Paris, to the provinces, and to the rest of Europe. Voltaire does not deny the importance of armies, but he interprets the supremacy of Louis XIV as ultimately a matter of cultural hegemony.

Playwrights, academicians, the masters of the French language, and the molders of the beaux-arts played a crucial part in the creation of this theater-state; and their leader was Molière. Voltaire presents him, of course, as the creator of the Comédie française, the supreme institution in the absolutist system of culture. But he also makes him out to be a "philosophe" and even a force in politics.[46] For it is Molière who writes the script of the new court culture. The performances of his plays set a tone for the court as a whole; and because the court is also a theater, they operate as plays within the play, spreading their influence in ever-widening circles. Voltaire describes the court production of *Tartuffe* in 1664 as the high point of a fête, which was the high point of the reign, which was the highest point of history.

In short, Voltaire presented the literary system of the ancien régime as a power system, a crucial ingredient of the Louisquatorzean state, and he placed Molière at the very heart of it—as the "the legislator of the manners of high society (*législateur des bienséances du monde*)."[47]

How does this highly inaccurate and anachronistic vision of history apply to Rousseau? Curiously, in light of the later antagonism between him and Voltaire, he accepted it. He subscribed to Voltaire's version of cultural history, but he saw it negatively rather than positively. Rousseau took culture to be the force that holds society together, the essence of politics, and therefore the source of all evil in the current social order. When he traced inequality back to its origins, he found it connected with the origins of language. When he followed the development of language, of literature, of the arts and sciences, he discerned a process of ever-increasing enslavement. The chains that bound mankind in the present had been forged by the finest artists in the world. To break those chains, therefore, the oppressed would have to turn against their culture; and they could not choose a better target for a cultural revolution than the classic French theater.

This theme runs through all of Rousseau's writing after the *Discours sur les sciences et les arts* (1750). It burst on him during the famous episode that he described in his *Confessions* (1782). In 1749, when he was an unknown scribbler, he walked from his garret in Paris to Vincennes on the outskirts of the city in order to visit Diderot, his friend and fellow hack, who had been locked up for publishing unorthodox and illegal books. As the sun beat down upon him, Rousseau pulled a journal from his pocket and read an announcement sponsored by the Academy of Dijon for the best essay on the topic, "Has the re-establishment of the sciences and arts contributed to the purification of morals?"

The question, as he described it later in the *Confessions*, literally knocked him off his feet and into a delirium. When he awoke, he found that it had cut to the heart of his existence. It had forced him to ask another, more troubling question: Who am I? And to face the answer: a Grub Street hack, an intellectual tramp, a literary flimflam man, living off handouts and odd jobs, trying to get operas performed and fiction published, working the salons in search of patrons and the cafés for contacts, living with a semiliterate plebeian wench, and abandoning her children to the orphanage—that is, probably to death. What had happened to him? What had become of the innocent boy who had begun life among the honest artisans of Geneva? He had been corrupted. How? By trying to win a place for himself as a man of letters—that is, by literature, by culture, by internalizing the code of the salons.

So when Rousseau wrote his answer to the question of the academy, he lashed out at culture itself—not just the arts and sciences, but culture in the broadest sense, as a way of life peculiar to the dominant classes of the ancien régime, or as he put it, "this uniform and perfidious veil of politeness . . . that we owe to the enlightenment ["Lumières'] of our century."[48] Enlightenment, the cause of the philosophes and the favorite game of the salons, was therefore bound up in a cultural system. When Rousseau pursued this thought to its logical conclusion a few years later, he broke with the philosophes; he drove a great wedge through the cause that he had joined; and he split his century in two.

How did he make the break? By an act of literary criticism, in his *Lettre à d'Alembert sur les spectacles*. This was the first and greatest act of deconstruction in the history of literature—greater than the deconstruction of Rousseau wrought by Jacques Derrida and Paul de Man. Rousseau took apart Molière's *Misanthrope* and transformed it into a manifesto for a cultural revolution. He accepted Voltaire's notion that the theater was the keystone to the culture of the ancien régime; then he turned it against the regime itself. Behind Jean Le Rond d'Alembert's article in the *Encyclopédie* proposing that a theater be erected in Geneva, he (rightly) spied Voltaire. Behind Voltaire, he perceived the entire literary system of France. And behind the literature, he saw a system of power—power embedded in language, in social codes, and in the behavior patterns of everyday life.

In short, Rousseau invented anthropology, and he did so as Freud invented psychoanalysis—by doing it to himself. Out of his introspection, his autobiographical obsession, he drew the insight that political systems are held together, are made to stick, by the force of culture. He transformed Voltaire's patrician view of literature into a democratic political theory; and he crowned his analysis of politics with a proposal for a civil religion, with republican festivals of the kind he placed in his imagination on the shores of Lake Geneva, at the opposite extreme from the sophisticated theatricality of the court of Louis XIV, but not far from what soon would take place in the street festivals of revolutionary Paris.

As it happened, the Revolution had room for both Voltaire and Rousseau. It put both of them in the Pantheon. Voltaire provided it with weapons against the Church (and against injustice in general, as in the Calas Affair), Rousseau with weapons against the aristocracy. But at the height of the Revolution, from August 1792 to July 1794, the Rousseauistic current swept everything before it. The Jacobins denounced Voltairean wit as a sign of "the aristocracy of the mind (esprit)," and Robespierre banished it from the Republic of Virtue.[49] They knew what they were doing, and it was serious business, nothing less than the reconstruction of reality. Therefore, they began with the task left to them by Rousseau: the rewriting of Molière.

4

CAREERS

Revolutionary Denouements

THE REVOLUTION TRANSFORMED the conditions of literary life in France. It ended censorship, destroyed the Book Trade Administration, dissolved the booksellers' guild, enacted a copyright law, abolished the Académie française, revoked the privileges of the official theaters, extinguished the system of patronage and protection based in the court, and drove most of the salon leaders into exile or hiding. The spectacular succession of events stimulated an enormous demand for news. From 1789 until 1799 more than 1,300 newspapers were created, and thousands of pamphlets poured from the newly freed presses. Book production declined, especially in the genres of fiction and belles-lettres, though the theater flourished (Marie-Joseph Chénier's *Charles IX* was an enormous success in 1789). A few writers like Bernardin de Saint-Pierre continued to command respect, and two academicians, Chamfort and La Harpe, led the attack on the academies, a favorite target of radicals like Marat. The Revolution created an intellectual pedigree for itself by putting Voltaire and Rousseau in the Pantheon, but it produced no great writers of its own. It guillotined the greatest poet of the century, André Chénier, the older brother of Marie-Joseph. And when the last of the surviving philosophes, Guillaume-Thomas-François Raynal, criticized the new order, it disowned him. The literary elite from the ancien régime was replaced by new men, who had languished in obscurity before 1789 and who seized control of the new media afterward. They were mainly journalists and pamphleteers: Jacques Pierre Brissot, Jean-Paul Marat, Jean-Louis Carra, Antoine Joseph Gorsas, Dominique Joseph Garat, Camille Desmoulins, Philippe François Nazaire Fabre d'Églantine, Elysée Loustalot, Jacques René Hébert, François-Noël Babeuf, Bertrand Barère, and even (in 1792) Robespierre.[1]

Morellet

A new tenor to cultural life set in with the institutional changes. It can be appreciated by a further reading of Morellet's *Mémoires*, allowing, of course, for its antirevolutionary bias. We left Morellet in 1788, enjoying retirement in a rich benefice and singing the praises of Loménie de Brienne. At that point Brienne's desperate attempt to save the ancien régime collapsed in failure, the Revolution exploded, and Morellet lost almost everything he had accumulated during the previous forty years. While the nationalization of church land deprived him of his priory, the new political order stripped him of his pensions. Soon he was reduced to the annuity of 1,275 L. left to him by Mme Geoffrin and, for company, to the last survivors of the salons.

Morellet held some radical ideas in 1788–1789. He wrote pamphlets in support of the doubling of the Third Estate and favored a constitutional monarchy. But by 1791 the Civil Constitution of the Clergy had destroyed his sympathy for the new order and deprived him of 95 percent of his income. He was then sixty-four years old and could safely withdraw into obscurity and silence. He cursed the Revolution in private when he paid his respects to the last of the grandes dames from the salons, the *maréchale* of Beauvau, the princess of Poix, the countess of Damas, and Mme d'Houdetot. They huddled together, widows, old women, and the aged abbé, damning everything about the new order.

What repelled Morellet above all was popular violence. He spent July 13 and 14, 1789, behind the windows of his apartment in the rue Saint-Honoré, staring out at a new phenomenon in the street below: the common people, massed in crowds, surging through the city, calling for blood, and seizing control of events. It horrified him, and he saw it again and again for the next ten years, both in the streets and in his dreams, as he recounted them in the *Mémoires*. Would the crowd break into his house and smash into his bedroom? The king's Swiss guards had been massacred only a few hundred yards from his residence during the uprising that overthrew the monarchy on August 10, 1792. When the September Massacres erupted three weeks later, he was leaving the house and a servant warned him, "Monsieur, one is massacring all priests at Saint-Firmin, at the Carmes, at the Abbaye, everywhere."[2] He turned back and shut himself inside for five days. At the height of the Terror in 1794, Morellet often heard the roar of the crowd gathered around the guillotine nearby at the Place de la Révolution (now

Place de la Concorde). When he crossed the street outside his house, he sometimes came upon cartloads of the condemned headed for the guillotine. On May 10, 1794, before he could avert his eyes, he saw a particularly terrible cartload (*fournée*): the count of Brienne and all his family, except his brother the former minister, who had just committed suicide, standing in the cart, their hands tied behind their backs, headed for death.

Haunted by such images, Morellet could do nothing more than withdraw into his room and write. He spilled his obsession onto paper, but he could not calm the fever in his brain, which steeped into his sleep. As he tossed in bed, he imagined hearing footsteps, muffled voices, a hand on the latch. He bolted from the sheets, gripping an imaginary dagger or collapsing on the floor. The nightmares became so insistent and the falls so dangerous that he finally strung a rope along the side of the bed to serve as a barrier. After throwing himself against the rope two or three times, he broke the spell. But he continued to vent his horror in his writing.

The main result, aside from the material incorporated in the *Mémoires*, was a macabre tract, "Le Préjugé vaincu, ou nouveau moyen de subsistance pour la nation, proposé au Comité de salut public en messidor de An 11 de la République" ("Prejudice overcome, or a new means of subsistence for the nation, proposed to the Committee of Public Safety in messidor of Year 11 of the Republic"). Adopting the voice of a loyal Jacobin, Morellet proposed a way to solve the subsistence crisis and to suppress the counterrevolution at one blow: the Committee of Public Safety should guillotine all suspects and feed their flesh to the starving masses. Further, it should require all citizens to buy guillotined meat from a

National Butchery, to be designed by Citizen David (Jacques-Louis David, the revolutionary painter and organizer of civic festivals), and it should force them to eat platters of the meat in a ceremony to be called "the true communion of patriots" or "the eucharist of the Jacobins."[3] Morellet derived the idea for this essay from Jonathan Swift's *A Modest Proposal* (1729), a dark, ironic proposal to solve the famine in Ireland by cannibalism. He never published it.

Two episodes in the *Mémoires* illustrate Morellet's view of the cultural dimension to the revolutionary conflict. The first concerns Morellet's attempt to save the archives of the Académie française. In destroying the Academy, the revolutionaries attempted to extinguish what they called "the aristocracy of the mind." They also wanted to wipe out the academicians, or at least their leaders, beginning with Marmontel, the Academy's perpetual secretary, who had gone into hiding in Normandy. After arresting Jean Pierre-Claris de Florian, an academician from the aristocracy, an agent of the Paris Commune told Morellet they were on Marmontel's trail, adding, "You academicians, you are enemies of the Republic."[4]

These circumstances left Morellet feeling exposed but also responsible, because he had taken over Marmontel's role of looking after the Academy's affairs. Before the "vandals," as he called the sans-culotte militants, could begin sequestering and destroying the Academy's materials, he slipped into its quarters in the Louvre and saved its "titles of nobility"—that is, its most precious treasures: the founding charter (*lettres patentes* of 1635), the minutes of its meetings, and the manuscript for the new edition of its dictionary.[5] The Academy had been working on the dictionary for thirty years and planned to dedicate it to Louis XVI. Along with the royal imprimatur, it was to bear the stamp of Voltaire, the supreme academician and champion of Louisquatorzean literature, who had devoted the last days of his life to perfecting the dictionary as the repository of the King's French. In 1793, however, the revolutionaries tried to "revolutionize language."[6] They replaced *vous* with *tu*, *Monsieur* with *citoyen*, and closed letters with "salut et fraternité" ("farewell and fraternity") instead of "votre très humble et très obéissant serviteur" ("your most humble and most obedient servant"). Morellet found such practices deeply upsetting, because they violated what he valued most—language itself, the basic stuff of culture. By rescuing the draft of the dictionary, he was attempting to save civilization.

He was thwarted, however, by one of the marginal writers from the ancien régime who had taken up a career as a Jacobin and secretary to the Paris Commune, Michel de Cubières. Having been mocked by the *Petit Almanach de nos grands hommes* for his prolix output of mediocre plays and poems, Cubières used his influence during the Revolution to dictate standards for a new kind of patriotic literature: no "religious fantasm," of course, and also no frivolity, no puns, no dedications to princes, no characters in plays except bourgeois and common people, no classicism of the kind advocated by Boileau—and no dictionary produced by the Académie française.[7] After learning that Morellet had absconded with the manuscript for the dictionary, Cubières demanded, in the name of the Commune, that he surrender it. Morellet complied, but he allowed himself to be drawn into a discussion about the unrepublican way in which the Academy had ruled over language. That confrontation made him nervous three weeks later, when he appeared before the General Council of the Paris Commune in order to receive a certificate of civism—that is, official confirmation of his support for the Revolution. The refusal of a certificate could lead to a trial before the Revolutionary Tribunal and the guillotine.

As recounted in the *Mémoires*, this second episode reads like a confrontation between Jacobinism and the Enlightenment. After sitting through several hours of sans-culotte oratory and patriotic songs, Morellet was summoned before the president's desk. The president, a certain Lubin who was the son of a butcher at the Porte Saint-Honoré, said he had received a warning that Morellet's *civisme* was suspect. The denunciation had come from Cubières, and it was supported by a sans-culotte militant named Vialard, who claimed that Morellet had written an apology for despotism fifteen or sixteen years earlier. Only afterward did Morellet realize that Vialard must have referred to his *Théorie du paradoxe* of 1775, which had ridiculed the outspoken journalist and enemy of the physiocrats, Simon-Nicolas Henri Linguet, by pretending to praise him as a champion of oriental despotism. Vialard had taken the message literally. Like some of Swift's readers, he could not recognize irony, and like the readers of the *Père Duchesne*, the crude, radical newspaper by Jacques René Hébert, who had taken up journalism after a failed career as a playwright before the Revolution, he expected political writing to come in bursts of undisguised emotion, *grandes joies* and *grandes colères*. Morellet had become acquainted with the sans-culotte way of reading in his own backyard, where he could hear a neighbor, the wife of a coachman named Gattrey, declaim from journals like

Le Père Duchesne to a group of working-class women in an adjoining courtyard. A regular spectator at the Jacobin Club and a passionate partisan of *sans-culottisme*, "femme Gattrey," as Morellet called her, read out passages and accompanied them with "harangues worthy of a fury released from hell."[8] Ten months later, she, too, denounced Morellet for incivism.

But when he stood before the Commune in September 1793, Morellet's main difficulty was to overcome the barrier of an alien way of reading that separated him from his judges and made his Enlightenment tracts unintelligible to them. He protested that everything he had written supported the cause of liberty—freedom of the press, free trade, and the free exercise of different religions. Vialard retorted that he had written in favor of despotism, so the president appointed a committee to look into Morellet's writings, and he named to it three solidly sans-culotte intellectuals: Jacques Bernard, a former priest and friend of Robespierre; Pierre-Louis Pâris, a university professor and enthusiastic Rousseauist; and Vialard himself, a hairdresser who was interested in questions of science and literature.

During the next week, Morellet met with one committee member after another, exhibiting his wares as a philosophe. First, he bearded Vialard. In order to make a favorable impression, he wore a frayed coat and arrived with a sack containing eight or more of his books, "intended to prove my civisme."[9] He displayed them one by one: his attack on the Inquisition, his plea for the tolerance of Protestants, his pamphlets against the monopoly of the East India Company, his writings in support of Voltaire and Turgot. Everything that emerged from the sack seemed to come straight from the heart of the Enlightenment.

Vialard did not make many comments, aside from an occasional "that is good" and "that is well." He appeared favorably impressed when Morellet said he had been punished for one of his pamphlets by imprisonment in the Bastille. Although he maintained his sternly republican demeanor, Vialard also seemed pleased to have been designated to judge an author who had written such impressive tomes. When he took them in hand, however, he contented himself with a quick look at the texts. For his part, Vialard specialized, he explained, in the study of mechanics. In his capacity as a hairdresser under the ancien régime, he had invented a new kind of wig and had presented the invention to the Academy of Sciences in the hope of obtaining some recognition. Having received none, he felt as resentful as Cubières (and also Jean-Paul Marat) toward the academicians who had dominated the cultural life of France.

In the face of the gulf that separated them, Morellet could hardly hope to win over this man by exhibiting his impressive bibliography. When he had laid out half of his works, Vialard interrupted him with an objection that brought them back to the heart of the matter.

But what you are showing me has nothing to do with the question at hand; you must prove your *civisme* during the *journées* of August 10 and May 31 [the uprisings that had overthrown the monarchy and purged the Convention of Girondists], and all of this does not prove it. To be sure, we know very well that some men of letters had fairly good sentiments in former times; but none of them has been visible since then, and all academicians are enemies of the Republic.[10]

Morellet had no answer to that objection, because, far from rallying to the cause of the people during the popular uprisings, he had shunned them with horror. He therefore emphasized that he had worked closely with Voltaire and Turgot in the past and that he was now too old to be an activist. Moreover, the Academy, he noted, included some members like Nicolas Chamfort and Jean-François de La Harpe who had supported the Revolution. Vialard did not give in: "But you must be a revolutionary from August 10th and May 31st. One can only give certificates to those who proved their *civisme* by their conduct during those two events; and neither you nor your academicians have done anything of the kind."[11]

Lacking a reply, Morellet put his books back in the sack and went home. The next day he presented his case to Bernard, the defrocked priest who had married and settled into sans-culotte territory, the faubourg Saint-Antoine. Once again Morellet spread out his literary productions and stated his arguments to prove that he had served the cause of liberty under the ancien régime. But Bernard, like Vialard, seemed incapable of understanding his prose. He opened the books, looked at the titles, and perused some passages while murmuring, "That is good, that is well, we shall see," all without showing much interest. Then, according to Morellet's account of their conversation, "He confronted me, as Vialard had done, with the terrible argument that I had not proven my *civisme* on August 10, nor on September 2 [the outbreak of the September massacres, when Parisians slaughtered many hundreds of suspected counterrevolutionaries], nor on May 31."[12] Again, Morellet gathered up his books and returned to the rue Saint-Honoré.

The next day he called on Pâris, the professor who represented the brains of the trio. Morellet refrained from carrying his sack of books, because he assumed that Pâris was familiar with his works inasmuch as he had taught literature at the Collège royal. As it turned out, the professor had not only read the *Théorie du paradoxe* but also understood perfectly well that it was an argument based on irony. Morellet hoped that he had finally entered friendly territory. "I said to myself that I was like the philosopher who had landed on an unknown beach and who found on it some geometrical figures traced in the sand: here is the sign of a human."[13] He felt even more reassured when Pâris said he intended to deal with the case at the next meeting of the Commune.

The session began with raucous speeches and songs. A sans-culotte struck up a sanguinary variation of the Marseillaise, and the audience rose to its feet, booming out the chorus. "Fuck it all, that bugger, he can really belt it out," people remarked as they took their seats, according to Morellet's description of the meeting.[14] Finally, those seeking certificates of *civisme* had their turn to appear, but before their cases were discussed, Vialard denounced the excessive indulgence with which some Parisian Sections had treated suspects. Seized with patriotic indignation, the Commune decreed that all certificates would be reexamined by newly designated committees before new ones could be considered. This decision threw into doubt everything Morellet hoped he had obtained in his interviews. But he subsequently realized that it probably had saved his life, because Vialard might have persuaded the Commune to refuse his certificate and send him to prison. Instead of taking immediate action, it postponed examination of his case along with the others, and he escaped the Terror by doing his best to remain as unnoticed as possible.

Having survived this confrontation with *sans-culottisme*, Morellet was called to testify about his civism once more in the wake of the denunciation by "femme Gattrey." He reported to the revolutionary committee of his Section at ten o'clock in the evening of July 15, 1794, less than two weeks before the fall of Robespierre and the beginning of the end of the Terror. The committee was composed of sans-culottes wearing Phrygian caps. Again, Morellet invoked all the works he had written in favor of liberty, and again no one seemed interested in his literary past. The committee members wanted to know exactly what he had done on August 10, 1792. He explained that he had visited some friends in the country but had returned to Paris on the following day. Since the uprising had provoked a massive flight of nobles, his response impressed his judges. Then, Morellet continued, "my interrogation became more strange." His case hung on a single question: "Why," I was asked, "were you gay before August 10 and have you been sad since then?"[15]

In Morellet's mind this question demonstrated the naivete of the sans-culottes. He succeeded in getting around it and saving his life. After Robespierre's fall, he no longer faced any danger. He lived in retirement throughout the rest of the Revolution, participated in the revival of the Académie française as part of the Institut de France in 1795, and died in 1819 at the age of ninety-one, celebrated as a survivor from a literary world that had long ago ceased to exist. His account of his experience, tinged as it is with his horror of the Terror, reveals something of what the Revolution meant for the sans-culottes. Their revolution was a matter of the heart, not the head. It was an *émotion populaire*, a succession of great days that gave the common people a chance to make history happen instead of being its victims. In asking Morellet where his heart was on August 10, 1792, the sans-culottes revealed the cultural distance that separated them from him. They did not reject the ideas of the Enlightenment, but they understood democracy in a new way, as a force that operated at street level.

Baculard d'Arnaud

Like Morellet, Baculard d'Arnaud kept a low profile during the Revolution, but he had no source of support other than his pen. He continued to churn out novels full of sentiment and lugubrious encounters with misery and morbidity. By 1780 that formula had worn thin, and in 1789 he turned seventy-one, yet he never stopped writing, right up to his death in 1805. He avoided politics, both in his daily life and in his publications, and he remained in obscurity, except for one moment of triumph, on May 14, 1790.

On that date, the Théâtre de la Nation, successor to the Comédie française, put on a performance of a melodrama d'Arnaud had published in 1764, *Les Amants malheureux, ou le comte de Comminges*. It was a hit. According to a review in *Le Moniteur universel*, the audience was carried away by "a pathetic wave that overcame the heart."[16] It went through twenty performances that year, two in 1791 and six in 1793, quite a success for that time.

As the "tenebrous genre" went, *Les Amants malheureux* could hardly be blacker. The stage was set as a crypt under a Trappist monastery, shrouded in darkness except for the light of one lantern. An open grave and skulls scattered about an altar summoned up the pervading sense of death. Suffering from a "too sensitive heart," the count of Comminges has renounced the world as a monk in the most austere of all orders, where speech was forbidden. He and his cousin Adélaïde had fallen passionately in love, but their fathers had chosen other spouses for them. While Adélaïde was condemned to a marriage against her will, Comminges withdrew in despair to the monastery, loving her more than ever. Her husband died, however, and she then joined the same monastery disguised as a man so that she could be near Comminges, though unknown to him and unable to speak with him. In the final act, all is revealed, accompanied by "torrents of tears" (the abbot has given Comminges permission to speak.) Both lovers, now fatally ill, are eager for death. Adélaïde collapses into the open grave, Comminges throws himself beside her, and they die together in an embrace.[17]

Because authors received a share of the box office receipts, the success of *Les Amants malheureux*, and the performance of another previously published play, *La Mort de Coligni*, provided d'Arnaud with some income. Yet he remained desperately poor. In 1791 he proposed selling all of his plays to the Théâtre de la Nation—or at least releasing his rights to them in exchange for a loan of 1,200 L.—because, he explained, he had fallen deeply in debt and was trapped in "a very dire situation."[18] That negotiation failed, and he fell back on writing still more novels.

He turned them out at an extraordinary rate, although all were variations on the same theme, *sensibilité*. By then the vogue for sentimentality had lost so much of its appeal that Chamfort remarked, "The rareness of a true sentiment has made me stop myself sometimes in the streets to watch a dog gnawing a bone."[19] Yet d'Arnaud continued to invoke "torrents of tears" in three novels published together in *Les Matinées* and four in *Les Loisirs utiles*, as well as *Lorimon, ou l'homme tel qu'il est* (1802) and *Eustasia* (1803). Their general tenor can be appreciated from *Géminvile et Dolimon, ou l'héroisme de l'amour et de l'humanité* (1799). Géminvile and Stéphanie, a married couple, love each other deeply, but suffer from such poverty that Géminvile insists on a divorce (a new possibility with the Revolution) so that Stéphanie can be rescued from destitution by marrying a rich man. When that possibility arises, she refuses, and he attempts to constrain her by committing suicide. At the last minute, they are rescued by Dolimon, who also loves her but heroically sacrifices his passion and shares his fortune with them so that they can be reunited. Along the way, d'Arnaud vents his resentment about wealthy acquaintances who refuse to loan money to the needy, and he invites his readers to weep over the happy ending: "Beneficent souls, souls worthy of your origin, steep yourselves in such a tender scene! Let your tears flow at the sight of this delicious tableau! May your sensitivity have pleasure at dwelling on it."[20]

In March 1793, Joseph de Mazelier, an aristocrat who had fled Paris and secretly returned, sought shelter with d'Arnaud and his wife. Despite the danger, they took him in and kept him alive for three months. On June 25 they were arrested. Mazelier was guillotined on the next day, and d'Arnaud remained in prison for two months, then released. Although the circumstances are obscure, this close call made d'Arnaud sink deeper into debt. The few references to him during the following years indicate that he and his wife moved from apartment to apartment, one cheaper than the other, ending up, according to one report, in an unheated attic. In fact, they spent their last years in an apartment at the Quai de l'École, and they managed to keep their furniture, although one creditor had threatened to seize it. D'Arnaud was often seen begging for *écus* in the Café de la Régence. He occasionally got free meals from a café in the rue Mouffetard, and in one of his last letters, dated February 7, 1803, he sounded desperate: "Four or five louis would at this time save my life. I have no wood [for heating] and barely enough food."[21]

D'Arnaud died on November 9, 1805, eighty-seven years old and destitute. By then he was known as "the dean of the poor devils."[22]

Pierre Manuel

When the Revolution broke out, the main occupation of Pierre Manuel was distributing pamphlets to peddlers from the printing shop of J. B. Garnery at 17 rue Serpente, where he lived in a spare room. The pamphlet trade was booming in the first half of 1789, and it depended on the peddlers whom Manuel described as a powerful political force: "This army of peddlers who dash out from the Quai des Augustins into streets and crossroads seems to force the common people to become informed and to discuss all the operations of the government, which no longer can keep its affairs secret. Their thousands of voices spread fame and animate the public spirit which alone is capable of overturning the ancient edifice of abuses."[23]

According to *Vie secrète de Pierre Manuel*, he cultivated the peddlers in order to launch his own political career. While hawking pamphlets and newspapers, they spread the word of his patriotism and helped him get elected as a member of the executive committee in his local district, Val-de-Grâce.[24] He presented himself as a "conqueror of the Bastille," although in fact he had not participated in its storming and was nearly strung up from a lantern after being mistaken for its governor on July 14.[25]

During those chaotic months, civic life remained fluid and power began to crystallize around new institutions, opening up possibilities for a new breed of politicians. The sixty districts created to administer the elections to the Estates General became local power bases linked to the Paris Commune, which with the mayor's office took over the government of the city as a whole. Manuel was selected by his district to represent it in the Commune, and on October 9 the Commune's General Assembly named him as one of several "administrative councilors" assigned to departments in the new municipal administration. Along with six others, he supervised the police department, and within it he assumed responsibility for the area he knew best—publishing, the book trade, and everything connected with the printed word. Although he did not function as a full-time, salaried official, his surveillance role gave him access to resources within the new power system.[26]

Manuel used his influence to promote the freedom of the press. It had been proclaimed as a matter of principle in the Declaration of the Rights of Man and of the Citizen on August 26, and it had existed in practice after July 14, when hundreds of newspapers appeared in defiance of the censorship.[27] Yet censors, police inspectors, and bureaucrats in the book trade administration still occupied their offices. Manuel did what he could to trim their powers, while the National Assembly began to redesign the rules that governed literary life, a complex process involving issues like libel, book privileges, and import regulations. When he intervened in the book trade, he gave free rein to pamphleteers, journalists, printers, booksellers, and peddlers. At one point, for example, a bookseller asked him to give permission for a work to be published. He refused on the grounds that an approval of the request would imply the possibility of refusing it, thereby contradicting the freedom of the press.[28]

At the same time, Manuel seized an opportunity for himself. He had access to the archives of the Bastille that were saved after its destruction. When he looked through them, he discovered a gold mine of information about subjects that once had occupied the underground press and now promised to fascinate readers in the new regime. The archives contained hundreds of dossiers revealing repressive measures by the police and the activities that the police tried to repress. Manuel selected the juiciest documents—reports of police spies, investigations by inspectors, interrogations of prisoners—and published them in a series of books: *La Bastille dévoilée* (1789–1790), 2 volumes; *La Police de Paris dévoilée* (1790), 2 volumes; and *La Chasteté du clergé dévoilée* (1790), 2 volumes.[29] He spent most of the first two and a half years of the Revolution producing these works along with a related publication, *Lettres originales de Mirabeau, écrites du donjon de Vincennes* (1792), 4 volumes. They created an enormous sensation, lifted him out of penury, and provided an opportunity for him to re-engage in politics on the radical Left.

When the Bastille fell, its archives were scattered. Some disappeared, some were sent to Catherine II in Russia, and many were recovered and deposited in the Hôtel de Ville. The new mayor of Paris, Jean Sylvain Bailly, claimed that those on deposit fell under his authority and appointed a team of commissioners to put them in order. But he soon came into conflict with the Commune, and one of his lieutenants gave Manuel the keys to several armoires in which they were kept. Manuel asserted that he had a right to the keys in his capacity as administrator of the book trade. He maintained, moreover, that the archives belonged to the nation, which had recovered its sovereignty in conquering the Bastille, whereas the former police, which had generated the documents, could no longer assert proprietorship over them, because the police had acted as agents of an arbitrary power that had lost all legitimacy. Indeed, it was his duty to publish the archives. They testified to the despotism under which the French had suffered, and they should be viewed as fundamental documents "to assure our new constitution."[30]

La Bastille dévoilée came out in six installments (*livraisons*), each of about 150 pages. When the first appeared, the *Mercure de France* hailed it as an important event, one that was certain to "arouse curiosity and gain attention. . . . The revelation of the mysteries of the Bastille is certain to interest everyone." Earlier works such as Linguet's *Mémoires sur la Bastille* had lifted much of the secrecy surrounding the Bastille, but the public had only a vague idea of who had been imprisoned and what had gone on inside its walls. Drawing on its actual registers, *La Bastille dévoilée* listed all the prisoners going back to 1663. In some cases, it included transcriptions of their interrogations and reports on how they had been hunted down and captured. A preface announced that some of the documents would be deposited in the Parisian Lycée, where anyone could verify their authenticity. The *Mercure* marveled that "one can see here, for the first time, a faithful picture of despotism, as it represented itself," and it congratulated the anonymous editor for his commentary on the documents: "His eloquence is animated by the most ardent patriotism; he has succeeded in accompanying the facts with bold and philosophical reflections."[31]

In order to make the most from this enthusiastic reception, Manuel rushed to get out the installments as quickly as possible. The first two brought the story up to 1762, along with some background material. The third installment jumped to the period 1782–1789, so that readers could get inside information about the latest, hottest events such as the Diamond Necklace Affair of 1785. Subsequent installations filled in the gap, and as Manuel drafted them, he modified his mode of exposition. Instead of limiting the entries to a few facts—the dates of a prisoner's entry and release, the reason for his arrest, and occasionally a transcription of a document—he described each case in an essay of his own that sometimes went on for many pages. In addition to the reports of the police, he drew on all sorts of material and sometimes asked the former prisoners to write the articles about themselves.[32] Manuel's friend

Jacques-Pierre Brissot wrote that the true reason for his *embastillement* was not his association with underground libelers as indicated in his dossier but rather his struggle to free the French from despotism. In his own entry, Manuel eliminated the information about secretly pirating Mirabeau and added a similar explanation: "I was one of the victims of despotism, because too soon I wanted to be one of the apostles of liberty."[33]

As he worked his way through the last five installments, Manuel added more editorial comments, sounding increasingly like a militant Jacobin. Indeed, he was one, having joined the Jacobin Club sometime in late 1789 and given a speech at its first public session on October 14, 1791. The later installments were full of diatribes against "that ancien régime where the most sacred rights of man and of justice were violated in the most odious and outrageous manner."[34] At the same time, Manuel began to add "separate items," which struck another note. They included police reports on brothels with the names of clients from the clergy and nobility and "anecdotes" about prelates who abused children in the private rooms of their palaces.

This sensationalism helped sales. By mid-1790 *La Bastille dévoilée* was in its third edition, and it had eclipsed a rival publication, *Mémoires historiques et authentiques sur la Bastille*, a three-volume work published in late 1789. The anonymous author of this book, Jean-Louis Carra, was a hack writer like Manuel, although he occupied a higher rung in the world of letters, having gained a position as a sub-librarian in the Bibliothèque du roi. He, too, had been pilloried by the *Petit Almanach de nos grands hommes*, and he used the same, violent rhetoric in serving up excerpts from a stash of the Bastille papers that somehow had come into his possession.[35] Manuel challenged the accuracy of the *Mémoires historiques et authentiques* at several points, and it ceased publication after it had reached 1775 in the chronology of its articles on the prisoners, so he won the race to dominate the demand for revelations about the horrors of the ancien régime.[36]

Manuel succeeded so well, in fact, that his accounts of the crimes frequently made the prisoners look worse than the police who arrested them. In installment after installment, Manuel recounted tales about swindlers, frauds, counterfeiters, libelers, smugglers, spies, gamblers, financiers, and all sorts of disreputable adventurers. He named names, even though, he acknowledged, their exposure could damage the honor of many families, or even make the police look good. "Now is the time to let everything come out; it is good to profit from it."[37]

After recounting an anecdote about a brothel run by a madam known as "la Baudouin" who was also a police informer, Manuel remarked that it would be possible to produce several volumes filled with such material—and that is just what he did after completing *La Bastille dévoilée*.[38] He failed to be reelected to the Commune in August 1790. Temporarily abandoning his career in Parisian politics, he retired to his hometown of Montargis with a load of notes and transcriptions (or possibly some of the original manuscripts) from the Bastille archives, and spent the next months producing a sequel, *La Police de Paris dévoilée*, this time with his name on the title page along with that of his printer, Garnery.

The new book resembled the previous one in style and tone—a mixture of moral indignation and sensationalism—except it was organized differently. Manuel divided the text into broad themes and wrote essays on each of them, quoting extensively from the Bastille papers, which included hundreds of dossiers compiled by the police. He began by describing the attempts of the police to control literature. Separate sections exposed the subservience of censors, the use of spies, raids on bookshops, the confiscation of book shipments, the repression of underground newsletters, the surveillance of theaters, and arrests of authors, including the French expatriates who operated out of London and Brussels. Manuel also discussed the policing of theaters, gambling, and the grain trade. But as the revelations accumulated, the subject that took up most space was sexual scandal.

Volume 1 contained a survey of monks arrested in brothels. It covered twenty-four monastic orders and stopped at that point only because, as Manuel put it, a longer account would become too repetitive. He proceeded, however, to discuss prostitution in general at much greater length with plenty of details about the women and their clients. In volume 2, Manuel took up the discussion of authors and prisons once again, but then offered another survey of prostitution that went on for 144 pages. It was a succession of "anecdotes" taken from police reports, for example:

> Demoiselle Vestris spreads herself thin. She has at the same time M. Brissart, M. Hocquart, M. de Sainte-Foy and a Venetian count. Her maxim is: "Either don't take on any of them or satisfy them all." But she also knows that a mouse who has only one hole is soon caught."[39]

Manuel wrote that he could publish twenty thousand more anecdotes of this type. He included so many that *La police dévoilée* read in places like a "chronique scandaleuse" from the libel literature of the ancien régime. In fact, one of those libels, actually titled *La Chronique scandaleuse*, was reprinted in 1791 with new material lifted from *La Police de Paris dévoilée* and an acknowledgment of Manuel.[40] Having learned the tricks of the trade in the literary underground before the Revolution, he had adapted them to a new career as a scandalmonger by making use of the opportunities that opened up in 1789. Of course, he did not want to appear as a libeler. In case the reader should suspect him of exploiting the public interest in scandal, he protested, "It is not the pleasure of bad-mouthing that has made me reveal everything shameful about the human species. It was necessary to show to what extent the corruption had advanced."[41] In fact, his revelations required "courage," he claimed. He wrote as a "philosophe whose duty it is to peer into hearts and viscera."[42] His mission was to warn the French that they had to reform their morals before they could create a successful new order. And he made the political implications of his moralizing clear by dedicating the book to the Jacobin Club.

Judging from a long, favorable review in the *Mercure de France*, *La Police de Paris* was received as Manuel intended. The reviewer treated it as a worthy successor to *La Bastille dévoilée*: "The first exposes despotism in all its horror, the second in all of its lowness."[43] The third book in the series, *La Chasteté du clergé dévoilée*, went back over a theme that had already received plenty of coverage in the first two: priests caught in brothels by the police. It recounted more than two hundred cases, all of them from the police archives. An index at the end listed the names of the clergymen so that readers could check on anyone they knew, and an introduction invited the readers to enjoy the sordid details: "Everything that corruption can invent that is the most immoral and the most indecent . . . is gathered together in this collection."[44] The text contained the police reports, guaranteed to be accurate, along with editorial comments, which appealed to the voyeuristic tastes of the readers.[45] As in the previous volumes, the author justified publishing such material as his patriotic duty. While exposing the decadence of the ancien régime (but without expressing any sympathy for the degradation suffered by the prostitutes), he claimed that he was reinforcing the resolution of the National Assembly to release monks from their vows and even, he hoped, to permit priests to marry.

Although the general character of *La Chasteté du clergé dévoilée* indicates that Manuel wrote it, drawing on the archives at his disposal, his authorship cannot be proven. *Vie secrète de Pierre Manuel* claimed he did. In fact, it accused him of blackmailing the archbishop of Bordeaux, Jérôme-Marie Champion de Cicé, who supposedly paid 3,000 L. to have his name expunged from the text, and it said Manuel made 12,000 L. by selling it to Garnery.[46] But the book appeared anonymously like a libel under a facetious address, "à Rome, de l'Imprimerie de la Propagande," and, perhaps because it was so lurid, Manuel did not claim it as one of his publications.

By contrast, Manuel trumpeted his authorship of the last of the works that he churned out during his months in Montargis, *Lettres originales de Mirabeau, écrites du donjon de Vincennes pendant les années 1777, 78, 79 et 80: Contenant tous les détails sur sa vie privée, ses malheurs, et ses amours avec Sophie Ruffei, marquise de Monnier* (1792) [Original letters of

Mirabeau, written from the dungeon of Vincennes during the years 1777, 78, 79 and 80: Containing all the details of his private life, his misfortunes, and his love affair with Sophie Ruffei, marquise of Monnier], 2 vols. As the title made clear, this was a sensational work. Mirabeau had become the most famous and flamboyant member of the National Assembly. After his death in 1791—and before the discovery of his secret correspondence with the king in 1792—he was mourned as a national hero and buried in the Pantheon. He had become a celebrity before the Revolution in large part because of his love affair with Marie-Thérèse-Richard de Ruffey, marquise of Monnier, the young wife of an old magistrate in Pontarlier near the château de Joux, where Mirabeau was confined by *lettre de cachet* for tempestuous behavior during family quarrels.

Owing to the prison's lax regime, he attended social occasions in Pontarlier. He met Mme de Monnier, overwhelmed her with his energy and his impressive, somewhat repulsive ("beau-laid") appearance, and ran off with her to Switzerland and then Holland. They were arrested in Amsterdam by agents of the French police in May 1777. While his mistress was shut up in a *maison de force*, Mirabeau was imprisoned in the dungeon of Vincennes. The police permitted them to correspond, although their letters were confiscated after being read. During the three years of his imprisonment, Mirabeau wrote two pornographic works, *Erotika Biblion* and *Ma Conversion* (later reprinted as *Le Libertin de qualité, ou confidences d'un prisonnier au Château de Vincennes*); and a powerful attack on despotism, *Des lettres de cachet et des prisons d'État*. Published after his release in August 1782, they added to his notoriety. So did his triumph at a spectacular trial.

Having been condemned to death for sedition and abduction, he turned himself in to the court in Pontarlier, defended himself with extraordinary eloquence, and had the sentence reversed with expenses charged to Mme de Monnier's husband. These and other adventures made Mirabeau the most visible member of the Estates General when it opened on May 4, 1789, and his oratory made him its most conspicuous leader at the time of his death on April 2, 1791.[47]

The papers that Manuel carried with him to Montargis included most of Mirabeau's correspondence with Mme de Monnier when they were confined in separate prisons. Manuel spent months transcribing the letters—arduous work, he explained in the introduction to the *Lettres originales*, but well worth it, because they revealed the greatest love story of the century. By following the exchanges between "Gabriel" and "Sophie," as Manuel called them, readers would enjoy an intimate view of "that passion that burned them even in their underground prison cells." They would get to know Mirabeau as a great lover: "There was not one fiber in his entire being that did not express the violence of his love." They would be able to imagine him when "he devoured her with a wildness that turned into fury." And they could thrill to her responses: "Then it was that she seemed to taste the supreme voluptuousness, then it was that she covered him with caresses, that she ate him with kisses." In short, Manuel invited his readers to enjoy an obscene and voyeuristic spectacle featuring the most famous leader of the Revolution.[48]

Whether or not the letters produced all the *frissons* promised by Manuel, they treated the public to an inside view of Mirabeau's love life. Readers learned of "Gabriel's" terms of endearment for "Sophie": "ma fanfan," "mimi," "chère amour," "divine amie." Along with complaints about the hardship of his confinement, Mirabeau's letters contained plenty of erotic passages: "We loved our bed so much! Ah! it was there that we often engaged in battles, although we never quarreled." "I bite you everywhere . . . feverish for your whiteness, I cover you with sucking."[49]

Manuel arranged to publish the four-volume work with Garnery, who had sheltered him during his lean years. They printed twenty thousand prospectuses and ran off five thousand copies in the first edition, which apparently sold out quickly and brought in an enormous profit. But it did not go over well with readers like André Chénier, who published a letter in the *Journal de Paris* condemning it for vulgarity and pretentiousness. Chénier excoriated Manuel as typical of the writers who had failed to gain recognition under the ancien régime and now filled the press with repulsive demagoguery.[50]

A more damaging objection came from Mirabeau's mother, who filed a criminal complaint, claiming that Manuel had violated her right to ownership of the manuscripts as her son's only heir. By May 1792 when the case came to trial, Manuel had reentered politics and had gained considerable power as *procureur* or public prosecutor of the Paris Commune. In his testimony, Manuel argued that all the papers of the former police belonged to the French people, who seized sovereignty on July 14, 1789. In publishing them, he had performed a great service for the nation. It was a heroic task, for he had labored twelve hours a day for ten months on a work that honored Mirabeau as a champion of liberty and an enemy of despotism.[51] Manuel did not mention his quarrel with Mirabeau, his relations with Mme de Nehra, and his secret pirating of a Mirabeau pamphlet before the Revolution. Instead, he claimed that Mirabeau would have approved of his publishing the letters, "because he wrote them to Love, and from love they must pass to Glory."[52] And he denounced the trial as an attempt by enemies of the people to silence him. At that time, the atmosphere in Paris had become so explosive that the magistrates backed away from a decision by transferring the case to a civil court, which dropped it after the overthrow of the monarchy ten weeks later.[53]

Having completed the marathon of editing and writing in Montargis, Manuel returned to Paris in July 1791. To promote the resumption of his political career, he published a final book, *Les Lettres de P. Manuel, l'un des administrateurs de 1789*, printed by Garnery, who again provided him with lodging. Writing as a "citizen philosopher," Manuel strung together a succession of open letters addressed to prominent figures: the king, the queen, the duke of Orléans, the archbishop of Bordeaux, Bailly, then mayor of Paris—and also to fellow patriots such as Brissot, Desmoulins, and the members of the Jacobin Club. All of the letters denounced enemies of the people or demanded radical measures. Manuel upbraided the count of Artois, Louis XVI's younger brother—"I have some truths to tell you"—and then excoriated him for emigrating: "The nation accuses you." He scolded the queen for having lost the affection of the people. He gave the pope a dressing down and, writing as the voice of the French people, ordered the French ambassador to the Vatican to tell him he was nothing more than the bishop of Rome.[54] Manuel would employ this confrontational rhetoric throughout the rest of the Revolution, notably in an open letter to the king, which began, "Sire, I don't like kings." [55]

Manuel's oratory can be traced through the speeches he gave at the Jacobin Club, all of them heavy on declamation and denunciation. On November 29, 1791, he summoned the Jacobins to mount a "crusade" against priests. On December 2, they applauded his election as public prosecutor of the Commune, and he declared, "May the will of the people be executed!" He presented a copy of *Les Lettres originales de Mirabeau* to the Jacobins on January 22, 1792, depositing it beside a bust of Mirabeau, where it was to be kept on display next to a framed copy of a *lettre de cachet* and a stone from the Bastille. On February 5, he read an open letter addressed to the ministers "to reproach them for their perfidiousness and to threaten them with the vengeance of the people." Ten days later he demanded "that one draw lots among the ministers to send one of them to the scaffold." Having established his credentials as a champion of the people, he was elected president of the Jacobins on June 14. [56]

Manuel's rise to power ran into difficulties, however, because after being elected prosecutor of the Commune on November 30, 1791, he was accused of being ineligible for the office. To qualify as a candidate, one had to be an "active citizen"—that is, to have paid the equivalent of three days' labor in taxes (7 livres, 7 sous in 1790), to have a fixed domicile in Paris, and to have enlisted for service in the National Guard. Manuel failed on all three counts, according to an attack on him published by Charles-Pierre Bosquillon. Although Manuel eventually earned a great deal from his publications, he had not collected the money in time to pay adequate taxes in 1790. His name did not appear in any register of the National Guard. And given the "well-known mediocrity of his fortune," as Bosquillon put it, he had not rented an apartment; he merely received free lodging from Garnery during the printing of his books. Just before his election, Bosquillon claimed, Manuel made a retrospective payment of taxes for 1789 and 1790, but that, too, was illegal.[57] Manuel dismissed these accusations as an effort by reactionaries to discredit him. As he was already exercising power with the backing of the Jacobin Club, he did not suffer political damage from attacks by the rising right-wing forces—those associated with the Feuillant Club formed by conservative constitutional monarchists who had seceded from the Jacobins in July 1791. On the contrary, the attacks reinforced his emergence as a leader of the new Left—Jacobins committed to the overthrow of the monarchy.

To follow Manuel's political career during the next two years would require a long excursion through the history of the Revolution. But his evolution as a politician can be appreciated by noting his role at a few turning points. The king's flight to Varennes, an unsuccessful attempt by Louis XVI to escape from the Revolution in June 1791, exposed a fatal flaw in the constitution drafted by the National Assembly: How could a constitutional monarchy succeed if the monarch disavowed the constitution? After being captured in Varennes, Louis was escorted back to Paris, where he became in effect a prisoner of the Revolution. During this crisis, a large crowd gathered at the Champ de mars to petition for his removal or the creation of a republic. Dozens of petitioners were massacred by the National Guard under the command of Lafayette, who was aligned with the Feuillants. Faced with the widening gap between the Left and Right, the Feuillant leaders persuaded Louis to accept a slightly revised constitution, which went into effect when the newly elected Legislative Assembly held its first session on October 1. Throughout this period, Manuel fired up passions on the Left by speeches in the Jacobin Club and his campaign to be elected prosecutor of the Commune. His defiance of the king—with the "Sire, I do not like kings" in an open letter that he read to the Jacobins on January 29, 1792—made him stand out as a leader of the Parisian radicals.

By this time, the Jacobins (with the notable exception of Robespierre) were agitating for a declaration of war against Austria. Manuel supported the campaign in favor of the war, which had the ultimate aim of overthrowing old regimes everywhere in Europe and the immediate goal of toppling the Feuillant ministers, who were committed to maintaining peace. In speeches to the Jacobins on February 5 and 12, 1792, he called for the "vengeance of the people" and even demanded stringing up the ministers on the gallows.[58] The Feuillants failed to maintain their support in the Legislative Assembly, which declared war on April 20. The French army, still organized according to the practices of the ancien régime, floundered in attacking the Austrian Netherlands and then fell back as the Prussians, who joined the Austrians, began to advance toward France's borders. While menaced from abroad, Parisians feared conspiracies at home. Aristocrats, priests, the king, the queen (now loathed as "the Austrian"), and secret agents in the overcrowded prisons were rumored to be preparing a counterrevolutionary insurrection. Radical sans-culottes in the Parisian Sections demanded that the authorities take action and threatened to do so themselves. As prosecutor of the Commune, Manuel, along with the mayor, Jérôme Pétion, was responsible for maintaining order, but he had to suspend his functions in early June while defending himself against the charge of criminal conduct in the publication of the Mirabeau letters. After his triumph in the trial and his election as president of the Jacobin Club on June 14, he was poised to play an active part in the political crisis.

Violence first erupted on June 20 in an invasion of the Tuileries Palace, where the king resided under the protection of Swiss guards, by a crowd of sans-culottes. Claiming to be peaceful protesters who demanded an audience, they forced their way into the royal chambers, surrounded the king, and required that he drink to the health of the nation while wearing a liberty cap. Louis complied, keeping his composure, and the sans-culottes eventually withdrew. But the Department of the Seine, a conservative body that contested the Commune's authority over the city, treated the incident as an attempted insurrection. It suspended Manuel and Pétion from their posts, claiming that they had organized the violence.

In a hearing before the Department's directors, Manuel and Pétion were charged with neglecting their duty, because they had failed to dispatch forces from the Hôtel de Ville to subdue the riot. In fact, Manuel had been seen in the Tuileries Gardens looking as if he supported it. But the Department failed in its attempt to have the two men dismissed. Supported by the Commune, they resumed their offices in late July, and Manuel was soon denouncing the king as "the source of all our suffering" in the Jacobin Club.[59]

In retrospect, the riot of June 20 looked like a dress rehearsal for the full-scale assault on the palace, which overthrew the monarchy on August 10. By the end of July, Manuel's violent speeches had earned him a reputation as a radical republican, cut from the same cloth as Robespierre, Desmoulins, and Danton, who then served under him as deputy prosecutor. They cultivated a power base among the sans-culottes in the Paris Sections. In fact, as mentioned, the term "sans-culotte," according to Mercier, originally referred to indigent writers like Nicolas Gilbert, who could not afford decent clothing.[60]

The Parisian sans-culottes included a large number of artisans and laborers along with radical bourgeois; and after the Sections were opened up to passive citizens in the summer of 1792, they dominated municipal politics. On August 1, news arrived of the Brunswick Manifesto, a declaration from the commander of the invading forces that anyone who harmed the king and his family would be summarily executed. The Sections reacted with fury. They began to meet night and day, convinced that sovereignty was invested in them and that they had to take direct action to save the Revolution. On the night of August 9, they sent delegates to an insurrectional Commune, which replaced the existing Commune but kept Pétion and Manuel in their functions. Reinforced by Fédéré troops who had arrived from Marseille, they stormed the Tuileries Palace on the next day. Although the king and his family had already taken refuge with the Legislative Assembly, the Swiss guards resisted, and more than a thousand on both sides were killed in a bloody battle.

The Legislative Assembly declared the king suspended and called for elections to decide on his fate and create a new constitution. Although moderates wanted to house the king and his family in some comfort in the Ministry of Justice, Manuel insisted, in the name of the Commune, that they be held in an austere tower of the Temple. He accompanied them in a carriage to their prison and visited them there at least twice during the next months, always addressing the king as Monsieur instead of Sire. Meanwhile, he cooperated with the Commune in adopting measures for the defense of Paris. The Prussian and Austrian armies continued their advance, picking off the fortresses on the French border. Longwy fell on August 23, Verdun on September 2, leaving nothing between the invading forces and Paris. Seized with fear and fury, Parisian militants enlisted to confront the enemy, but rumors spread that the counter-revolution would explode as soon as they left the city and that it would be triggered by traitors in the prisons. In a speech before the Legislative Assembly at midday on September 2, Danton, now minister of justice in the provisional government, called for direct action to save the country by destroying its enemies. The tocsin rang, and sans-culottes, accompanied by Fédérés, began to butcher suspects trapped in prisons. The slaughter continued until September 6. More than a thousand persons were killed, most of them priests, prostitutes, and common criminals.

As prosecutor of the Commune, Manuel had authority over the prisons and could not avoid some complicity in the massacres. In a speech to the Jacobin Club on November 5, he claimed that he had attempted to stop the slaughter: "Standing on top of a pile of bodies, I preached respect for the law." All of Paris, he argued, was compromised in "those moments of desolation." At that point Collot d'Herbois, a more radical Jacobin, interrupted him to protest that the violence was necessary to save the nation and that September

2 should be recognized as "a great *journée* of which it [the nation] was the instrument."[61]

Although Manuel's activities during those five tragic days cannot be known with any precision, he certainly saved some lives. The most revealing account of a rescue comes from the memoirs of Mme de Staël, who was already famous as the daughter of Necker, the leader of a literary salon, and the wife of the (then absent) Swedish ambassador. She did not know Manuel, but while studying a list of the members of the Commune, she recounted, "I suddenly remembered that Manuel, one of them, had some connection with literature and that he had published the letters of Mirabeau with a preface, which in truth was badly done but which showed the ambition to demonstrate some talent." She obtained a private audience with him two days before the outbreak of the massacres and, playing on his pride at being solicited by a great lady of the salons, persuaded him to release two of her aristocratic friends from prison. On September 2, she, too, attempted to escape the slaughter. She set out in a carriage drawn by six horses with footmen in livery, hoping to impress the crowds by a display of her eminence. Instead of letting her pass, they seized the carriage and took it to the Hôtel de Ville. Manuel then sheltered her in his office and, late at night, in the midst of the massacres, escorted her back to her house in a carriage of the Commune. On the next day he sent her a passport, which made it possible for her to reach Switzerland in safety. Manuel was capable of magnanimity, she wrote, and he also was "susceptible to being won over by his vanity."[62]

From September 2 to 10, 1792, elections were held for the National Convention, which assembled on September

20. On the same day, the French army, reinforced by its new recruits, turned back the Prussians at the Battle of Valmy. The French went on to defeat the Austrians at Jemappes on November 6, freeing the country from the danger of invasion for the rest of the winter. The Convention immediately abolished the monarchy and then faced the question of what to do with the king. Having established a reputation as an outspoken enemy of monarchs, Manuel was elected as a deputy from Paris and was identified at first with radicals like Danton and Robespierre, who had cooperated with him throughout his term as prosecutor. (He had attended Desmoulins's wedding on December 29, 1790, in the company of Robespierre, Brissot, and Mercier.) But he soon drifted toward the moderate faction known as Girondins. He spoke less frequently in the Jacobin Club and stopped attending its meetings by the end of the year. When the trial of the king, now known as Citizen Louis Capet (Manuel liked to call him "Louis the last"), began on December 3, Manuel had no difficulty in voting him guilty of treason. Like other moderates, however, he could not bring himself to vote for the death penalty. During the debate, he favored holding a national referendum on the fate of the king. When that proposition failed, he voted against the king's execution and explained that he preferred to have Louis kept in a secure prison until he could be banished—preferably to the United States, as Manuel had recommended a few days earlier in the *Journal de Paris*.[63]

The decision for the death penalty on January 17, 1793 carried by only one vote. Acting as secretary to the session, Manuel had tabulated the votes; and when the verdict was announced, he suddenly rose from his seat, saying he had to leave the hall to get a breath of fresh air. He was later accused of taking the voting record with him so that he could modify it. Although in fact he did not dare to make such an attempt, his defiance of the Convention's decision made him look like a renegade to the Jacobin Left. On the day after the vote, he resigned as a deputy, saying he would return to a quiet life in Montargis. His enemies claimed that he had no right to leave his post and that a resignation was a form of treason. But the Convention accepted it, and Manuel disappeared from the political scene.[64]

When he arrived in Montargis, however, he ran into the hostility of the local Jacobins. At a meeting to draft recruits for the army on March 14, he defied the town authorities, and a riot broke out, taking him as its target. He was badly beaten and nearly lynched. After a long period of recovery, he found shelter in the town of Ablon near Fontainebleau. Meanwhile, France was torn apart by a succession of disasters: an uprising in the Vendée area south of Nantes; incipient revolts in several cities; the defeat of the French army at Neerwinden on March 18 and the defection of its general Charles François Dumouriez to the Austrians; disarray among the Girondins, who were associated with Dumouriez; the growing dominance in the Convention of the radical Montagnards, led by Robespierre and Danton; and the threat of another insurrection by the Parisian sans-culottes, who were infuriated by soaring bread prices and persistent rumors of counterrevolutionary conspiracies. A violent crowd from the Sections overwhelmed the Convention on May 31 and again on June 2. It forced the Convention to take extreme measures, beginning with the purge of the leading Girondin deputies. By fits and starts and jolts of violence, the Revolution had entered a new phase, which came to be known in retrospect as the Terror.

Considered as an accomplice of the Girondins, Manuel was arrested near Fontainebleau on August 21 and imprisoned in the Parisian Abbaye. The Convention had proscribed twenty-one Girondin deputies nearly a month earlier. Most of them were tried by the Revolutionary Tribunal on October 24 and guillotined on October 31. Manuel's trial did not take place until November 13. Identified as a "man of letters," he was charged with inciting the September Massacres, attempting to save the former king, and other offenses. Various witnesses testified that they had heard him express royalist sympathies and that he had tried to falsify the vote to execute Citizen Capet. Although he forcefully rebutted the accusations, he was declared guilty on November 14 and guillotined the same day.[65]

Manuel was not the only revolutionary from the lower ranks of writers to be eliminated at the first stage of the Terror. Other previously unsuccessful authors—Brissot, Carra, Gorsas, Louvet de Couvray—had developed new careers as journalists and politicians after 1789, only to be cut down in 1793. (Although Louvet was purged with the Girondists, he survived until 1797.) They would be followed by more marginal figures from the ancien régime who threw themselves into the Revolution and then were devoured by it—Jean-Paul Marat, Georges Danton, Camille Desmoulins, Philippe Fabre d'Églantine, Jean-Marie Collot d'Herbois, Jacques Hébert, and others. Of course, the Revolution recruited leaders from many sectors of society, including aristocrats like Lafayette, Condorcet, and Lepeletier de Saint Fargeau; and the counterrevolution had its share of hacks such as Isodore

Langlois, Barnabé Farmain de Rozoi, and Jean-Pierre Gallais. No straight line led from the garret to the Jacobin Club, nor did political engagement simply result from frustrated ambition. Ideological commitment, personal connections, opportunism, and other factors contributed to the complex pattern of revolutionary careers. The case of Manuel, who is rarely even mentioned in histories of the Revolution, cannot be taken to demonstrate an argument about causality. It illustrates something different: the cultural revolution at work within the French Revolution, a force propelled by the fusion of print and politics. The poor devils from the old world of letters provided much of the energy that made this combination so explosive. During their struggle to survive in Grub Street, they acquired the experience and the passion that made them so effective in the struggles for power after the collapse of the ancien régime.

CONCLUSION

ASE STUDIES have the advantage of filling abstract interpretations with concrete detail, but they are necessarily arbitrary. The lives of André Morellet, François-Thomas-Marie de Baculard d'Arnaud, and Pierre Louis Manuel illustrate the nature of literary careers at three levels within the world of letters. They have been chosen because they can be fully documented, both under the ancien régime and during the Revolution. The lives of other writers might reveal different patterns, if enough evidence could be uncovered. Yet the three cases have enough in common to support some conclusions about the writer's lot during those crucial years of French history.

They show how the general conditions of literary life—the need to win protectors, the scramble for sinecures and pensions, the underdeveloped character of the book trade, the power of the police, the constraints of privilege (in the academies as well as the booksellers' guild), and the social barriers that kept outsiders outside the salons—were actually experienced by writers at a time when literature occupied a crucial place in public affairs. Although literature had already figured in the power system developed under

Louis XIV, it emerged in the mid-eighteenth century as a force that appealed to a broad public. Voltaire epitomized it. His celebrity, reinforced by the renown of other writers, attracted acolytes from younger generations—so many, in fact, that the world of letters suffered from a population problem. The number of writers more than doubled—it may nearly have tripled—between 1750 and 1789.

The pressure created by this growth played out in different ways. While producing all sorts of tracts, Morellet fought off competitors for sinecures and finally landed a benefice that seemed certain to provide for him in his old age—until the Revolution snatched it away. D'Arnaud failed in the competition for the highest stakes, but succeeded well enough to survive by selling sentimental novels and extracting loans from friends. Manuel's attempts to win acclaim from legitimate publications got nowhere and drove him into underground activities—peddling pornography, organizing clandestine publications, and spying for the police. His experience illustrates the importance of Grub Street as an element of the literary landscape.

Conspicuously absent from the three stories was the assumption that a writer could live by his pen. D'Arnaud managed to make a living, meager as it was, but his example illustrated the precariousness of such an existence, and like the others, he tried hard to secure a pension or an appointment to a well-paid position. Although the marketplace for books expanded greatly after 1750, it did not function in a way that freed writers from dependence on patronage and protections. Copyright did not exist. Publishers purchased manuscripts from authors, sometimes for a few thousand livres, often in return for an allotment of copies of the printed book. But they did not pay royalties or enough for a writer to sustain a respectable existence, especially if he had a family, and their own incomes were undermined by the prevalence of piracy, which by 1770 accounted for more than half the books on the domestic market.[1]

The case studies demonstrate the continuing importance of patronage and the different ways it operated. A patron might be an aristocrat, who hired a writer as a tutor to his children; a grandee in Versailles, who took him on as a secretary; a royal mistress, who gave him a pension attached to the income from a privileged journal; or the king, who named him to an office such as royal historiographer. There were many emoluments, but the supply was limited, and the demand increased as the number of writers grew. How could an ambitious lad who arrived from the provinces make his talent known? Fabre's play, *Les Gens de lettres*, dramatized the difficulties. Although an epigram published in the *Mercure* could serve as a calling card, the beginner needed introductions. They were often arranged by other men of letters, who could open a door to a salon or provide access to actors in the Comédie française. The actors, however, commonly underpaid and humiliated authors, and their decisions involved intrigues, which could extend all the way up to the courtiers (*gentilshommes de la chambre du roi*) charged with the ultimate authority over the privileged theaters.[2]

Success in this difficult game required *protection* or string pulling. Voltaire was an active protector himself, eager to recruit beginners like d'Arnaud and Jean-François Marmontel for his "church" and to find positions for them among his contacts in *le monde*. The art of networking was explained in *Conseils d'un vieil auteur à un jeune, ou l'art de parvenir dans la République des lettres* (Advice by an old author to a young one, or the art of getting ahead in the republic of letters) (1758). First, make contacts: "I would advise a young man who aspires to literary honors to begin by getting attached to some friends who can make him appear talented." Then gain entrance to the salons: "A name praised by a pretty mouth is certain to command respect." And persevere with the help of protectors: "Under the aura of powerful protections, you will overcome the obstacles that act as a barrier."[3]

Of course, talent was crucial for advancement. The careers of Marmontel and Morellet showed that enough mobility existed within the world of letters to accommodate gifted young men from obscure backgrounds. In such cases, they usually got their start from within the Church. Not only did the Church provide them with a basic education, but it also served as the only available channel for pursuing an intellectual vocation. They went to seminaries, found employment as teachers in religious establishments, and frequently received tonsure as abbés. After reading philosophic tracts, they abandoned the path to the priesthood. But the Church was a key institution that led to the rise of the writer as a public figure by the end of the century.

The century ended with the prestige of writers at its zenith. They had been celebrated, pantheonized, and canonized in what has come to be known as "le sacre de l'écrivain" (the coronation or apotheosis of the writer).[4] By 1789 writers had begun to replace priests as a source of moral authority—not everywhere, but in the view of an increasingly secularized reading public, particularly the lawyers and other professional men who would be elected to the Estates-General. After the excesses of the Reign of Terror, a reaction set in. The early romantics inspired a religious revival. But there was no turning back to the ancien régime, because the Revolution destroyed the foundation of the old world of letters—the system of privileges that extended from books themselves to the booksellers' guild; the administration of the book trade, journals, theaters, academies; and the sinecures dispensed by patronage. Some of those institutions, including salons, were revived after 1815. But the Restoration could not restore the fundamental structures and attitudes that had fashioned literary careers before 1789.

Career patterns also illustrate the way the Enlightenment converged with the Revolution. The convergence was far more complex than the adoption of Enlightenment principles in manifestos like the *Declaration of the Rights of Man and of the Citizen*. Although it assumed many forms, the process can be appreciated by reconsidering the opposition of Voltaire and Rousseau as it was understood at the time. By transferring their remains to the Pantheon, Voltaire in 1791, Rousseau in 1794, the revolutionaries created an intellectual pedigree for themselves.[5] Voltaire provided them with intellectual weapons in their attacks on the Church during the early phases of the Revolution. Rousseau inspired the egalitarianism of the later phases. Morellet's confrontation with the sans-culottes—his attempt to pass as a patriot by displaying his publications to them—indicated an incompatibility between the Voltairean Enlightenment and the radical Revolution; and Robespierre's denunciation of the philosophes in the Jacobin Club expressed the same opposition. Wit, refinement, and *politesse* appeared as symptoms of counterrevolution in 1793–1794.

Those qualities were crucial for success as a writer under the ancien régime—for writers in general and philosophes in particular. Voltaire celebrated them in charting a course for the Enlightenment as a civilizing process driven by *gens de lettres* in alliance with gens du monde. For Rousseau, civilization, epitomized by literature, led to corruption and enslavement. When he broke with the philosophes, he denounced literature as a core ingredient of the power that held French society together.

That power was culture. The complexity of French culture cannot be reduced to Rousseau's diagnosis of it. But the Rousseauism of Robespierre and the other radicals of 1793-1794 shows how literature fed into a phenomenon that marked history at the end of the eighteenth century and is still alive today: the mobilization of ideas and passions in the form of a cultural revolution.

NOTES

ACKNOWLEDGMENTS

INDEX

NOTES

Introduction: Paths to Grub Street

1   See my article "The High Enlightenment and the Low-Life of Literature in Prerevolutionary France," *Past and Present*, no. 51 (May 1971): 81-115.

2   See *The Darnton Debate: Books and Revolution in the Eighteenth Century*, ed. Haydn Mason (Oxford, 1998), vii; Roger Chartier, *Les Origines culturelles de la Révolution française* (Paris, 1991), 102; Sarah Maza, *Private Lives and Public Affairs: The Causes Célèbres of Prerevolutionary France* (Berkeley, CA, 1992), 4; Darrin McMahon, *Enemies of the Enlightenment: The French Counter-Enlightenment and the Making of Modernity* (New York, 2002), 28; and Geoffrey Turnovsky, *The Literary Market: Authorship and Modernity in the Old Regime* (Philadelphia, 2010), 130.

3   On these and related themes, see my collection of essays, *The Literary Underground of the Old Regime* (Cambridge, MA, 1982) and "The Facts of Literary Life in Eighteenth-Century France" in *The Political Culture of the Old Regime*, ed. Keith Michael Baker (Oxford, 1987), 261-291.

4   See Jeremy Popkin, "Robert Darnton's Alternative (to the) Enlightenment"; Daniel Gordon, "The Great Enlightenment Massacre"; Elizabeth L. Eisenstein, "Bypassing the Enlightenment: Taking an Underground Route to the Revolution"; and Thomas E. Kaiser, "Enlightenment, Public Opinion and Politics in the Work of

Robert Darnton" in *The Darnton Debate: Books and Revolution in the Eighteenth Century*, ed. Haydn T. Mason (Voltaire Foundation, 1998). I replied to most of those objections in the last chapter of the book, "Two Paths through the Social History of Ideas."

5 "The Brissot Dossier," *French Historical Studies* 17 (Spring 1991): 159–205. Vincent Millot, the editor of Lenoir's papers, which I had consulted in manuscript form in 1965, agrees that Lenoir's remarks about Brissot's spying are credible: Millot, *Un Policier des Lumières* (Seyssel, France, 2011), 396, 652, and 1032.

6 "The Grub Street Style of Revolution: J.-P. Brissot, Police Spy," reprinted in *The Literary Underground of the Old Regime*, 68.

7 "The High Enlightenment and the Low-Life of Literature in Prerevolutionary France," reprinted in *The Literary Underground of the Old Regime*, 36.

8 "High Enlightenment and Low-Life," 40.

9 Norman Hampson, *Will and Circumstance: Montesquieu, Rousseau and the French Revolution* (Norman, OK, 1983).

10 See François Furet, *Penser la Révolution française* (Paris, 1979) and Keith Michael Baker, *Inventing the French Revolution: Essays on French Political Culture in the Eighteenth Century* (New York, 1990).

11 I have developed this argument at length in a book that synthesizes much of my earlier research: *The Revolutionary Temper: Paris, 1748– 1789* (New York, 2023).

12 André Besson, *Contrebandiers et gabelous* (Paris, 1989), 207, quoted by Dominique Varry, "Pour de nouvelles approches des archives de la Société typographique de Neuchâtel," in *The Darnton Debate*, 235.

13 After thorough research for his *Enemies of the Enlightenment*, Darrin McMahon uncovered only a few hack writers who supported the counterrevolution after 1789.

14 Bibliothèque nationale, nouvelles acquisitions françaises, 10781. After imprisonment in the Bastille for writing libels in 1752, Jean Zorozabel Aublet de Maubuy survived as a minor writer until the early nineteenth century. His works included *Histoire des troubles et des démêlés littéraires, depuis leur origine jusqu'à nos jours inclusivement* (Amsterdam, 1779), 2 vols. and *Les Vies des femmes illustres de la France* (Paris, 1766), 6 vols. I have transcribed all the police reports, which can be consulted on my website, Robertdarnton.org.

15 Undated police report in Millot, *Un Policier des Lumières*, 1033.

16 Denis Diderot, *Le Neveu de Rameau* in *Œuvres* (Paris, 1951, Bibliothèque de la Pléiade), 396. Diderot shifts at several points from the economic to the psychological effects of living in poverty on the margin of cultivated society: see for example pp. 469–470.

17 *La Rameïde* ("Petesbourg," 1766), 25. See André Magnan, *Rameau le neveu: Textes et documents*, 2nd ed. (Paris, 2023).

18 "A Pamphleteer on the Run" in *The Literary Underground of the Old Regime* (Cambridge, MA, 1982), 71–121.

19 Milliot, *Un Policier des Lumières*, 1034.

20 See the fundamental study by Alain Viala, *Naissance de l'écrivain: Sociologie de la littérature à l'âge classique* (Paris, 1985).

21 The play contained some defiant remarks about buying nobility and the honor of peasant commoners, yet its happy ending suggested the ease of overcoming social tensions, even in the case of a *mésalliance:* Jean-Marie Collot d'Herbois, *Le Paysan magistrat, comédie en cinq actes et en prose* (Paris, 1780), 14, 20, 69, and 72.

22 *Billaud-Varenne membre du Comité de salut public: Mémoires inédits et correspondance. Accompagnés de notices biographiques sur Billaud-Varenne et Collot d'Herbois*, ed. Alfred Begis (Paris, 1893), 2.

23 Billaud-Varenne, *Le dernier coup porté aux préjugés et à la superstititon* (London, 1789) and *Despotisme des ministres de France, combattu par les droits de la nation, par les lois fondamentales, par les ordonnances, par les jurisconsultes, par les orateurs, par les historiens, par les publicistes, par les poètes, enfin par les intérêts du peuple et l'avantage personnel du monarque* (Amsterdam, 1789), 3 vols.

24 Desmoulins, *Le Vieux Cordelier de Camille Desmoulins*, no. 5 (Paris, 1834 reprint), 104 and 122. Denouncing Hébert directly, Desmoulins asserted, "Tu distribuais tes contremarques, et on m'assure que les directeurs se plaignaient de la recette" (110).

25 Desmoulins to his father, October 8, 1789, in *Correspondance inédite de Camille Desmoulins, député à la Convention nationale*, ed. M. Matton (Paris, 1836), 43.

26 Louis Antoine de Saint-Just, *Organt, poëme en vingt chants* ("Au Vatican," 1789), 2 vols., quotation from vol. 1, p. 3. *Arlequin-Diogène* appears in *Œuvres de Saint-Just: Discours-rapports, Institutions républicaines, Organt, Esprit de la Révolution, proclamation, lettres* (Paris, 1946).

An undated letter from Saint-Just to Desmoulins from April or May 1790 (325–326) indicates that they were friends who came from the same area near Laon.

27   See Jean Cruppi, *Un avocat journaliste au* XVIII*e siècle: Linguet* (Paris, 1895) and Darline Gay Levy, *The Ideas and Careers of Simon-Nicolas-Henri Linguet: A Study in Eighteenth-Century French Politics* (Urbana, IL, 1980).

28   Simon-Nicolas-Henry Linguet, *Le Fanatisme des philosophes* (London, 1764).

29   Linguet republished his attacks on Gerbier and the Ordre des avocats du Parlement de Paris in *Appel à la postérité, ou recueil des mémoires et plaidoyers de M. Linguet pour lui-même contre la Communauté des avocats du Parlement de Paris*, a 484-page collection of documents in his *Collection complète des oeuvres de M. Linguet* (n.p., 1779). See particularly his *Représentations au roi*, p. 150, where he denounced the "odieux despotisme" of the Order as a threat to "toutes les classes de la société."

30   Linguet developed his political theory most fully in *Théorie des lois civiles ou principes fondamentaux de la société* (London, 1767), 2 vols. Because he rejected the idea of natural law and argued in favor of the absolute power of monarchs as it existed in Asia, he gained a reputation as an advocate of oriental despotism. In *Esprit et génie de M. Linguet, avocat au Parlement de Paris* (London, 1780), he connected his view of absolutism with scorn for writers who cultivated the "Grands": 133.

31   Linguet, *Annales politiques, civiles, et littéraires du dix-huitième siècle* (1777), 2:322.

32   Linguet, *Annales politiques* (1779), 6:386.

33   Jacques-Pierre Brissot de Warville, *Un Indépendant à l'ordre des avocats, sur la décadence du barreau en France* (Berlin, 1781), 1. Brissot defended Linguet as a champion of liberty and a victim of the "despotisme" of the Order of Parisian lawyers (40). Then he went on, in Linguet's manner (47), to condemn corporate bodies in general, arguing "d'ouvrir au mérite la voie des dignités, des honneurs."

34   *Mémoires de J.-P. Brissot*, ed. Claude Perroud (Paris, 1912), 1:96.

35   There is no good biography of Gorsas, but the main course of his career is covered in the notice about him in *Dictionnaire des journalistes 1600–1789*, ed. Jean Sgard (Oxford, 1999), 2:787–789.

36 Antoine-Joseph Gorsas, *L'Âne promeneur, ou, Critès promené par son âne: Chef d'oeuvre pour servir d'apologie au goût, aux moeurs, à l'esprit, et aux découvertes du siècle* ("à Pampelune," 1786), quotations from pp. 10 and 36. In other pamphlets of the series, notably *Promenades de Critès au salon* (London, 1785), Gorsas occasionally interrupted Critès's buffoonery to praise serious art such as David's "Serment des Horaces." On the sociopolitical aspects of this anti-academic art criticism, see Thomas E. Crow, *Painters and Public Life in Eighteenth-Century Paris* (New Haven, CT, 1985), and on Gorsas's seditious use of satire, see Antoine de Baecque, *Les Éclats de rire: La culture des rieurs au XVIIIe siècle* (Paris, 2000), 235–287.

37 Lenoir included a police report on Gorsas in a draft of his memoirs, which I quoted in "The High Enlightenment and the Low-Life of Literature" (reprinted in *The Literary Underground of the Old Regime* (Cambridge, 1982), p. 26.) It appears in Milliot, *Un Policier des Lumières*, 1033.

38 See the excellent biography by Stephan Lemny, *Jean-Louis Carra (1742–1793), parcours d'un révolutionnaire* (Paris, 2000), and the police report on Carra in Milliot, *Un Policier des Lumières*, 1032.

39 Gérard Walter, *Marat* (Paris, 1933) argues that Marat was well off and even had aristocratic pretensions under the patronage of the comte d'Artois but fell into relative poverty and illness after that patronage ceased in 1783 (49–51).

40 *Découvertes de M. Marat, docteur en médecine et médecin des gardes-du-corps de Monseigneur le comte d'Artois, sur le feu, l'électricité et la lumière, constatées par une suite d'expériences nouvelles qui viennent d'être vérifiées par MM. les commissaires de l'Académie des sciences*, 2nd ed. (Paris, 1779), quotations from pp. 14 and 70. Marat's bitterness showed through his appeal to the public: "Mais comme il n'est au monde aucune société savante dont le jugement puisse rendre vrai ce qui est faux et faux ce qui est vrai, je crois qu'en me refusant sa sanction, l'Académie des sciences ne saurait changer la nature des choses. S'il faut être jugé, que ce soit donc par un public éclairé et impartial: c'est à son tribunal que j'en appelle avec confiance, ce tribunal suprême dont les corps scientifiques eux-mêmes sont forcés de respecter les arrêts" (6). Marat listed the subfields of his "péroptrique" in *Notions élémentaires d'optique* (Paris, 1784), 11.

41 Marat to Philippe-Rose Roume de Saint-Laurent, November 20, 1783, in *La Correspondance de Marat recueillie et annotée par Charles Vellay* (Paris, 1908), 28.

42 Marat, *Les Charlatans modernes, ou lettres sur le charlatanisme académique* (Paris, 1791), 7.

43 For biographical information on Mairobert, see *Dictionnaire des journalistes*, 2:787–789; Robert S. Tate, *Petit de Bachaumont: His Circle and the Mémoires secrets* (Geneva, 1968); and *The "Mémoires secrets" and the Culture of Publicity in Eighteenth-Century France*, ed. Jeremy Popkin and Bernadette Fort (Oxford, 1998).

44 *Mémoires secrets pour servir à l'histoire de la République des lettres en France* (London, 1784), 14:9–10, entries for April 2 and 3, 1779. These notices were written by Mairobert's collaborator and successor, Barthélemy-François Moufle d'Angerville.

45 Quotations from Mairobert's dossier in the archives of the Bastille, ms 11 683, folios 52 and 55.

46 *Mémoires secrets*, 14:9.

47 *Discours du citoyen David, député de Paris, sur la nécessité de supprimer les académies* (Paris, 1793), 1.

48 Henri Jean-Baptiste Grégoire, *Rapport et projet de décret, présenté au nom du Comité de l'instruction publique, à la séance du 8 août* (Paris, 1793), quotations from pp. 4, 8, and 10. Grégoire referred to the Republic of Letters on p. 3: "Il existe une république la plus ancienne de l'univers et qui doit survivre à toutes les révolutions; c'est la république des lettres. Par quelle fatalité les satuts de la plupart de nos corps académiques sont-ils une infraction aux principes qu'elle révère? Ils établissent une sorte d'hiérarchie entre les hommes qui ne doivent reconnaître que celle des talents." See also Sébastien-Roch Nicolas Chamfort, *Des académies, par S. R. N. Chamfort, de l'Académie française* (Paris, 1791).

49 Grégoire, *Rapport et projet de décret*, 10. Earlier attacks on the academies concentrated on their exclusivity as corporate bodies and their subservience to despotism. See Chamfort, *Des Académies* (Paris, 1791).

50 The 1762 edition of the *Dictionnaire de l'Académie française* defined "auteur" as "Celui qui a composé un livre, qui a fait quelque ouvrage d'esprit, en vers ou en prose." It defined "écrivain" as "Un auteur qui compose quelque livre."

51 *De la littérature et des littéraires* (Yverdon, Switzerland, 1778), 38.

52 Voltaire, *Le Pauvre Diable, ouvrage mis en vers aisés, de feu Mr. Vadé* (Paris, 1758), esp. p. 4. The scorn for writing for money, expressed notably by Nicolas Boileau-Despréaux and directed against Pierre Corneille, was widespread in the seventeenth century, when the writer (*écrivain*) emerged as a distinct social type pursuing a career within the realm of polite society: see Alain Viala, *Naissance de l'écrivain* (Paris, 1985).

53 Geoffrey Turnovsky, *The Literary Market: Authorship and Modernity in the Old Regime* (Philadelphia, 2009).

54 Voltaire, *Le Siècle de Louis XIV* (Paris, 1957; first edition 1751), see especially chap. 25.

55 Doigny du Ponceau, *La Dignité des gens de lettres: Pièce qui a concouru pour le prix de l'Académie française en 1774* (Paris, 1774), 2.

56 *De la littérature et des littérateurs*, 9.

57 Herbert Dieckmann, *Le Philosophe: Texts and Interpretation* (Philadelphia, 1948).

58 See Didier Masseau, *L'Invention de l'intellectuel dans l'Europe du XVIIIe siècle* (Paris, 1994). In a persuasive reassessment of the Enlightenment, Antoine Lilti insists that the intellectual as a social type did not emerge until the era of the Dreyfus Affair: *L'Héritage des Lumières: Ambivalences de la modernité* (Paris, 2019), 360–368 and 438–439. Although the argument may merely turn on a matter of definition, I think it valid to understand Voltaire as a model intellectual—that is, a man of letters who used his literary standing to attack the dominant values of his time.

1. Careers: The Ancien Régime

1 Among the many studies of eighteenth-century French writers, I have found the following to be most helpful: Lucien Brunel, *Les Philosophes et l'Académie française au dix-huitième siècle* (Paris, 1884); Maurice Pellisson, *Les Hommes de lettres au XVIIIe siècle* (Paris, 1911); Jules Bertaut, *La Vie littéraire au XVIIIe siècle* (Paris, 1954); Paul Bénichou, *Le Sacre de l'écrivain, 1750–1830* (Paris, 1973); John Lough, *Writer and Public in France from the Middle Ages to the Present Day*

(Oxford, 1978); Didier Masseau, *L'Invention de l'intellectuel dans l'Europe du XVIIIe siècle* (Paris, 1994); Daniel Roche, *Les Républicains des lettres* (Paris, 1988); Darrin McMahon, *Enemies of the Enlightenment: The French Counter-Enlightenment and the Making of Modernity* (New York, 2002); and Geoffrey Turnovsky, *The Literary Market. Authorship and Modernity in the Old Regime* (Philadelphia, 2009).

2　See Alain Viala, *Naissance de l'écrivain: Sociologie de la littérature à l'âge classique* (Paris, 1985). On Voltaire, I have relied especially on René Pomeau, *Voltaire en son temps* (Paris, 1995), 2 vols.

3　The phrase "le roi Voltaire," popularized by Arsaune Houssaye, was attributed by him to Frederick II of Prussia in answer to a question, "Quel est le souverain que vous craignez le plus en Europe?": Arsaune Houssaye, *Le Roi Voltaire* (Paris, 1860), 13.

4　Jean-François Marmontel, *Mémoires*, ed. John Renwick (Clermont-Ferrand, Franking, 1972), 1:80.

5　Marmontel, *Mémoires*, 1:313.

6　Marmontel, *Mémoires*, 1:313–315. Marmontel accompanied this remark with an account of the sinecures and pensions that made him wealthy.

7　The following case study is a reworked version of an essay that I first published in *André Morellet (1727–1819) in the Republic of Letters and the French Revolution*, edited by Jeffrey Merrick and Dorothy Medlin (New York, 1995), 5–38. Because this case study is an attempt to understand Morellet's career, it emphasizes concrete questions about his income and protections rather than his ideas and literary talent. But it is not meant to minimize the latter, which were crucial for his success and can be appreciated in other studies, notably Daniel Gordon, "'Public Opinion' and the Civilizing Process in France: The Example of Morellet," *Eighteenth-Century Studies* 22 (1989): 302–328; Dorothy Medlin, "André Morellet, Translator of Liberal Thought," *Studies on Voltaire and the Eighteenth Century* 174 (1978): 189–202; Dorothy Medlin, "André Morellet and the Idea of Progress," *Studies on Voltaire and the Eighteenth Century* 189 (1980): 239–246; and Auguste Mazure, *Les Idées de l'abbé Morellet* (Paris, 1910). A subsequent study by William H. Sewell, Jr., "The Abbé Morellet between Publishing and Patronage," in Sewell, *Capitalism and the Emergence of Civic Equality in Eighteenth-Century France*

(Chicago, 2021), 181–199, confirms my interpretation, but another contests it: Daniel Gordon, *Citizens without Sovereignty. Equality and Sociability in French Thought, 1670–1789* (Princeton, NJ, 1994).

8   André Morellet, *Mémoires de l'abbé Morellet de l'Académie française sur le dix-huitième siècle et sur la Révolution*, ed. Jean-Pierre Guicciardi (Paris, 1988), 41.

9   Morellet, *Mémoires*, 54.

10   Morellet, *Mémoires*, 55.

11   Morellet, *Mémoires*, 56.

12   Morellet, *Mémoires*, 66.

13   Morellet, *Mémoires*, 81.

14   Morellet to A. R. J. G. G. de Sartine, June 15, 1760, *Lettres d'André Morellet*, ed. Dorothy Medlin, Jean Claude David, and Paul LeClerc (Oxford, 1991), 1:3.

15   Morellet, *Mémoires*, 106. Six months was a slip for six weeks.

16   Morellet, *Mémoires*, 102.

17   Morellet, *Mémoires*, 136.

18   *Viaggio a Parigi e Londra (1766–1767): Carteggio di Pietro e Alessandro Verri*, ed. Gianmarco Gaspari (Milan, 1980), 102.

19   Morellet, *Mémoires*, 65.

20   Morellet, *Mémoires*, 65.

21   Morellet, *Mémoires*, 65.

22   Diderot to Sophie Volland, August 23, 1769, in his *Correspondance*, ed. George Roth and Jean Varloot (Paris, 1955–1970), 9:120.

23   Morellet, *Mémoires*, 139.

24   In arguing against an anachronistic view of eighteenth-century literature, I do not mean to imply that writers lacked a sense of vocation. On the contrary, Morellet, like many of the philosophes, believed that by guiding public opinion, writers ultimately determined the progressive course of history. He did not treat his polemical works as mere propaganda, even when he made it clear that they were aimed at the enemies of his protectors and that he expected to reap a reward for writing them.

25   Morellet, *Mémoires*, 161.

26   Morellet, *Mémoires*, 164–165.

27   Morellet, *Mémoires*, 166.

28   Morellet, *Mémoires*, 168–169.

29 André Morellet, *Théorie du paradoxe* (Amsterdam, 1775), quotation from p. 7; Morellet, *Mémoires*, 200–204.

30 Morellet, *Mémoires*, 206.

31 Morellet, *Mémoires*, 241: "Ce travail assez considérable devint, comme presque tous mes ouvrages, la proie des libaires: un volume in-octavo, de plus de 400 pages, fut entièrement perdu pour moi." See also the similar remarks on the sale of his translation of Beccaria: "Cette traduction, faite avec tant de soin, et si répandue en si peu de temps, ne m'a valu presque rien, attendu la grande habilité des libraires et la grande ineptie des gens de lettres, ou du moins la mienne, en matière d'intérêt" (150). Morellet's letters to the Société typographique de Neuchâtel (scattered through *Lettres*, 1:295–521), however, suggest that he was not so naive about the economics of publishing as he pretended to be in his memoirs.

32 Morellet to Pietro Verri, November 20, 1771, *Lettres*, 1:153.

33 Morellet, *Mémoires*, 271.

34 Morellet, *Mémoires*, 272.

35 These figures do not include the 1,000 L. pension on the Abbey de Tholey that Morellet received for overseeing the education of La Galaizière, which was raised to 1,200 L. in 1759, because he lost it after some complex ecclesiastical intrigues in 1770. The "indemnité" of 4,000 L. was raised to 6,000 L. in 1769 and then converted into a firm pension by Anne Robert Jacques Turgot, but Joly de Fleury cut it to 3,000 L. in 1782. It was meant to cover Morellet's expenses for work on the *Dictionnaire de commerce*, which included a salary of 1,500 L. that he paid to his secretary and payments for a copyist. In his memoirs Morellet did not mention the payments he received from the publishers of the *Dictionnaire de commerce*, which must have dried up after he failed to produce the copy. He continued nonetheless to receive a subsidy from the government for the *Dictionnaire* for twenty years, until it was cut off by the Revolution. On his arrangement with the Etienne brothers, Jacques and Robert, see Morellet to Turgot, November 29, 1768, *Lettres*, 1:102. The publishers apparently collected 250 subscriptions at 120 L. each after they published the prospectus in May 1769. Both they and Morellet's protectors seem to have complained about his inability to complete the task. He defended himself as best he could by insisting on how

much he wrote at the behest of the government, but he described his failure to produce the dictionary as "le tort de ma vie littéraire": *Mémoires*, 163–169. He discussed these problems in several letters to Turgot from 1768 to 1776.

36 Morellet, *Mémoires*, 270.

37 Morellet to Cesare Bonesana, marquis of Beccaria, January 3, 1766, *Lettres*, 1:45.

38 Morellet to Turgot, December 25, 1779, *Lettres*, 1:146–48.

39 Morellet to Shelburne, May 10, 1783, *Lettres*, 1:487. See also the similar remarks in Morellet's letter to Shelburne of October 27, 1782, *Lettres*, 1:468: "Vous savez à combien de ministres et de gens en place j'ai été attaché sans fruit."

40 Morellet to Turgot, December 23/24, 1768, *Lettres*, 1:104–105.

41 Morellet to Turgot, September 23, 1770, *Lettres*, 1:145–46.

42 Morellet to Turgot, December 25, 1770, *Lettres*, 1:147.

43 Morellet to Turgot, September 10, 1773, *Lettres*, 1:207.

44 Morellet to Turgot, September 10, 1773, *Lettres*, 1:207.

45 Morellet to Turgot, August 11, 1775, *Lettres*, 1:262–263.

46 Morellet to Turgot, September 11 or 18 (date is unclear), 1775, *Lettres*, 1:282.

47 Morellet, *Mémoires*, 220.

48 Morellet, *Mémoires*, 223–34.

49 The following account draws on d'Arnaud's correspondence published online (https://doi.org/10.13051/ec-bio/baculfranc 000871) as *Enlightenment Biographical Dictionary: François Thomas Marie de Baculard d'Arnaud*; on his extensive publications; and on contemporary sources such as *Mémoires secrets pour servir à l'histoire de la république des lettres en France* and Grimm's *Correspondance littéraire*, but it makes no pretension to originality and relies heavily on the biography by Robert L. Dawson, *Baculard d'Arnaud: Life and prose fiction* (Banbury, UK, 1976), published as volumes 141 and 142 in *Studies on Voltaire and the Eighteenth Century*. For information on d'Arnaud's finances, the account also draws on Bertran de la Villehervé, *François-Thomas de Baculard d'Arnaud: Son théâtre et ses théories dramatiques* (Paris, 1920).

50 Villehervé, *Baculard d'Arnaud*, 8.

51 D'Arnaud's dossier in the Bastille indicates that the police also suspected him of producing "quelques couplets satiriques contre

la cour." Louis Jean Félix Ravaisson-Mollien, *Archives de la Bastille* (Paris, 1881), 12:210.

52 For a full contemporary account of the case and the public's fascination with it, see Edmond-Jean-François Barbier, *Chronique de la Régence et du règne de Louis XV (1718-1763)* (Paris, 1857), 4:54-61 and 107.

53 Baculard d'Arnaud, *Les Époux malheureux* (Paris, 1803), 115. This reprint was faithful to the original 1745 edition, except in its ending, which d'Arnaud rewrote to make it turn out happily. By that time the annulment of the marriage had been reversed.

54 D'Arnaud, *Les Époux malheureux*, 121.

55 D'Arnaud, *Les Époux malheureux*, 159.

56 Dawson, *Baculard d'Arnaud*, 78-79 and 682-688.

57 In a rare reference to a payment, Joseph d'Hémery, the police inspector of the book trade, noted in his journal on July 15, 1751, that d'Arnaud had received 2,000 L. for an edition of his *Oeuvres diverses* from the Parisian bookseller Durand: Dawson, *Baculard d'Arnaud*, 163.

58 *Fanny, histoire anglaise* in *Oeuvres de M. d'Arnaud* (Paris, 1772), quotations from 1:78 and 17.

59 Dawson, *Baculard d'Arnaud*, 273.

60 *Salisbury* in *Nouvelles historiques* (Maastricht, 1785), 125.

61 *Norston et Suzanne, ou le malheur* in *Oeuvres de M. d'Arnaud* (Paris, 1784), III, 9.

62 *Mémoires secrets*, July 2, 1767; and Villehervé, *François-Thomas de Baculard d'Arnaud*, 44-45.

63 Robert Dawson made a heroic effort to identify first editions and published a list that runs for more than 100 pages: Dawson, *Baculard d'Arnaud*, 609-712.

64 *Correspondance littéraire, philosophique et critique par Grimm, Diderot, Raynal, Meister, etc.*, ed. Maurice Tourneux (Paris, 1879), 7:479. See the similar sardonic remark (9:185) about d'Arnaud's appeal to a popular public: "Il a beaucoup de vogue parmi les couturières et les marchandes de modes, et s'il peut mettre les femmes de chambre dans son parti, je ne désespère pas de sa fortune."

65 In *Fanny*, d'Arnaud spoke out against "l'autorité des grands, qui écrasent toujours sous leurs pieds et avec impunité les petits" (49).

But his sympathy for the downtrodden did not lead to criticism of the privileges and hierarchical order of the ancien régime.

66 Charles Monselet, *Les Oubliés et les dédaignés: Figures littéraires de la fin du 18e siècle* (Alençon, France, 1857), 2:157–72, and 168.

67 As explained in the introduction, I think Brissot's prerevolutionary career best exemplifies the hard lot of writers at the bottom of the literary world. Rather than repeating that argument here, I have chosen to do a case study of his friend Pierre-Louis Manuel, who also aspired to win glory as a philosophe and had to fall back on compromises and hack writing.

68 The only biography of Manuel, *Pierre Louis Manuel 1753–1793: Du pouvoir à l'échafaud* (Gien 2006) by Huguette Leloup-Audibert, does justice to his origins in Montargis but is rather thin on his prerevolutionary career. See also the articles on him in Auguste Kuckzinski, *Dictionnaire des Constitutionnels* (Paris, 1917), 2:427–427; and L. G. Michaud, *Biographie universelle, ancienne et moderne* (Paris, 1820), 26:541–544. *Vie secrète de Pierre Manuel* (n.p., n.d.) has suggestive details about Manuel's youth, but it is a crude libel produced during the repression of the Girondists in 1793, and it cannot be treated as a reliable source.

69 In a report on Manuel's imprisonment in the Bastille, the *Mémoires secrets* of February 11, 1786, noted, "Un M. Manuel ayant perdu son état de gouverneur des enfants de M. Tourton par la sortie violente qu'un certain abbé Royou avait fait contre lui dans *L'Année littéraire*, en le représentant comme un impie, comme un homme abominable, avait été obligé pour ressource de se faire libraire ou colporteur, a été aussi arrêté."

70 *Essais historiques, critiques, littéraires et philosophiques, par M. Ma....* (Geneva, 1783), quotations from pp. 9 and 80. Manuel also seemed to refer to his own experience in lamenting the lot of an author forced to make a living as a tutor (41).

71 *Coup d'oeil philosophique sur le règne de Saint-Louis: Par M. Manuel* ("À Damiette," 1788), quotations from pp. 5 and 8. Manuel ended the book abruptly with a reference to the work of abbé Louis-Pierre Saint-Martin, *Les Établissements de Saint Louis, Roi de France* (Paris, 1786), noting, "Son travail me dispense de continuer mes recherches" (164).

72   *Correspondance littéraire*, 14:394. However, the *Mémoires secrets* of April 30, 1786, praised the *Coup d'oeil* for being "hardi, satirique, plaisant."

73   *Lettre d'un garde du roi, pour servir de suite aux mémoires sur Cagliostro* (London, 1786), 5. In the *Correspondance littéraire*, 14:372, Meister dismissed the *Lettre* in a footnote: "Les critiques de ce pamphlet sont beaucoup plus amères qu'elles ne sont piquantes et spirituelles."

74   The source of the following account is a dossier in the National Archives, W 295, no. 246, supplemented by the entry on Manuel in Frantz Funck-Brentano, *Les Lettres de cachet à Paris: Étude suivie d'une liste des prisonniers de la Bastille (1659–1789)* (Paris, 1903), 415.

75   Funck-Brentano, *Les Lettres de cachet*, 415.

76   On Mirabeau's relations with Mme de Nehra, see Louis de Loménie, *Les Mirabeau: Nouvelles études sur la société française au XVIIIe siècle* (Paris, 1889), vol. 3, chap. 10. This study does not, however, mention Manuel's role in Mirabeau's pamphleteering.

77   *La Bastille dévoilée, ou recueil de pièces pour servir à son histoire* (Paris, 1789), 3:105–106. The brief notice on Manuel identifies him as "né à Montargis, fils d'un marchand de toile"; notes that he was suspected of writing the *Lettre d'un garde du roi*; and adds that he was "accusé de vendre plusieurs livres défendus, tels que les ouvrages de M. de Mirabeau, et d'envoyer en province des nouvelles à la main." The *Mémoires secrets* of February 12, 1786, noted that besides the *Lettre*, Manuel had written "beaucoup d'autres pamphlets." And in a report on his release from the Bastille, dated May 14, 1786, it claimed, "Il se loue de la douceur avec laquelle il y a été traité."

78   Lenoir papers, Bibliothèque municipale d'Orléans, ms 1422, "Sûreté"; and ms 1423, "Mélanges." Lenoir intended to work his notes and essays into a book but never completed it. They have been published with an excellent study of Lenoir and the Parisian police by Vincent Milliot: *Un Policier des Lumières* (Seyssel, France, 2011), which includes Lenoir's remarks on Audouin and Manuel (655–656 and 1033). Milliot interprets Lenoir as a conscientious administrator whose testimony can be trusted, although it expressed his horror of the Revolution, and he confirms my view that Manuel and Brissot were police spies.

79   On my argument, based on Lenoir's papers, that Brissot probably was a police spy, see "The Grub Street Style if Revolution: J.-P.

Brissot, Police Spy," *Journal of Modern History* 40 (1968): 301–327. And on the debate it provoked, see "The Brissot Dossier," *French Historical Studies* (Spring 1991), 17:191–205.

80 *L'Année française, ou vie des hommes qui ont honoré la France, ou par leurs talents, ou par leurs services, et surtout par leurs vertus: Pour tous les jours de l'année* (Paris, 1789), 2:v. In fact, Manuel included favorable notices on François I and Colbert, and he avoided anticlerical remarks; so, he did not expose himself to the fate of Sylvain Maréchal who was imprisoned for his *Almanach des honnêtes gens* (1788), which honored philosophers in place of saints and therefore was condemned and burned. The censor who approved the privilege for Manuel's book, which was dated August 28, 1788, noted, "Le but de l'auteur est raisonnable, ses principes sont sains."

81 *Le Petit Almanach de nos grands hommes* (n.p., 1788), 120.

82 *Supplément à la nouvelle édition du Petit Almanach des grands hommes, ou lettre à Messieurs de Rivarol et de Champcenets, par un des grands hommes du Petit Almanach* (n.p., 1788), 12.

83 *Lettre d'une Muséenne à M. Manuel, auteur du Supplément au Petit Almanach des grands hommes* (n.p., n.d.), 2 and 4. The *Musée* was a cultural organization open to everyone, where obscure writers could read their work before audiences that attended its sessions every Wednesday. Louis Sébastien Mercier, who was one of its members, described it as a non-privileged forum in contrast to the exclusive Académie française: "Musées" and "Le Musée de Paris," *Tableau de Paris*, ed. Jean-Claude Bonnet (Paris, 1994; reprint based on editions from 1782 to 1789), 1:1469–1470 and 2:1279–1280. Mercier consistently defended writers who pursued careers outside the circles of the literary elite. See "La littérature du faubourg Saint-Germain et celle du faubourg Saint-Honoré," in *Tableau de Paris*, 1:1211–1213; and *De la littérature et des littérateurs* (Yverdon, Switzerland, 1778).

84 *Dictionnaire des Conventionnels 1792–1795*, ed. A. Kuscinski (Paris, 1916), 2:428.

2. The Facts of Literary Life

1 *Almanach des beaux-arts contenant les noms et les ouvrages des gens de lettres, des savants et des artistes célèbres qui vivent actuellement en France*

(Paris, 1752). The following discussion is based on all the known editions of the *Almanach des beaux-arts* and its successor, *La France littéraire*, which were consulted in the Bibliothèque nationale and the university libraries of Princeton and Göttingen. Éric Walter consulted the 1784 edition of *La France littéraire* in order to estimate the number of writers that existed in the entire century (3,500) and during the period 1750–1789 (2,500), but he does not provide much evidence for those estimates and does not discuss the problematic nature of *La France littéraire* as a source: "Les auteurs et le champ littéraire," in *Histoire de l'édition française: Le livre triomphant 1660–1830* (Paris, 1984), 2:512. For further information on almanacs and related sources, see Daniel Roche, *Le Siècle des Lumières en province: Académies et académiciens provinciaux, 1660–1789* (Paris, 1978), 2 vols.

2 The full title was *La France littéraire ou almanach des beaux-arts, contenant les noms et les ouvrages des gens de lettres, des savants et des artistes célèbres qui vivent actuellement en France*. In the preface, Duchesne emphasized that he would include all authors, even those who wanted to be excluded, and explained, "Il y a aussi des gens de qualité qui cherchent à briller dans la République des lettres et qui rougissent ensuite de se voir sur la liste des auteurs, comme si la science dégradait la noblesse."

3 Bibliothèque nationale de France, nouvelles acquisitions françaises 10782, entry for La Porte.

4 *Mémoires secrets pour servir à l'histoire de la République des lettres en France* (Paris, 1784–1789), entries for Dec. 22, 1779, and June 7, 1762. See also the entries for Jan. 4, 1762; April 14, 1779; and Dec. 13 and 14, 1779; and the obituary of La Porte in the *Mercure de France*, Jan. 15, 1780.

5 The remark appears in Jean-François La Harpe, *Correspondance littéraire adressée à son altesse impériale Mgr. le Grand-Duc, aujourd'hui Empereur de Russie* (Paris, 1801–1807), 5:140. See also La Harpe, *Correspondance*, 3:44, for another version of the remark and a caustic description of La Porte as "le fripier le plus actif de notre littérature." Françoise Weil found evidence to suggest that du Tertre left *La France littéraire* in 1755 after a quarrel with its publisher over payment for his work: see her article on du Tertre in Jean Sgard, ed.,

Dictionnaire des journalistes, 1600–1789 (Grenoble, 1976), 1:368–369. It may be, therefore, that La Porte compiled the edition of 1756, although the preface to that edition does not mention a change in authorship. The first such reference comes in the preface to the edition of 1757, where La Porte, writing anonymously, said he had taken over "la continuation de cet ouvrage commencé en 1752 par M. Du Port du Tertre à qui ses occupations n'ont pas permis d'y travailler plus longtemps."

6   *Supplément à la France littéraire* (Paris, 1778), ii: "Avec ces trois volumes [the two-volume edition of 1769 and the supplement of 1778] on connaîtra tous les gens de lettres qui ont vécu en France depuis le commencement du siècle jusqu'à présent. . . . On saura leurs noms, leurs qualités, le lieu de leur naissance, souvent même leur âge, et pour connaître véritablement l'état de la littérature française depuis un siècle, il faut consulter ce livre nécessairement et l'avoir souvent à la main."

7   *Correspondance littéraire, philosophique et critique par Grimm, Diderot, Raynal, Meister, etc.*, ed. Maurice Tourneux (Paris, 1877–1882), 5:39; and *Journal de Paris*, July 8, 1778.

8   Voltaire to Marie Louise Denis, April 3, 1769, letter 14598 in *Voltaire's Correspondence*, ed. Theodore Besterman (Geneva, 1961), 71:214. See also letters 12658 and 14581.

9   *Second Supplément à La France littéraire de l'année 1758, pour les années 1760 et 1761* (Paris, 1762), v.

10 For example, entries from the edition of 1758 included Jean Arnault, a curate in Niort and author of an *Oraison funèbre de M. de Foudras*, an abbé Esnault from Sées who had published a *Dissertation sur l'histoire de Séez [sic]*, and a doctor from Salins named Clerc who had written a *Mémoire sur la goutte*.

11 On this theme, see Roche, *Le Siècle des Lumières*.

12 Le Grand to the Société typographique de Neuchâtel, April 14, 1780, in the dossier of Le Grand, papers of the Societé typographique, Bibliothèque publique et universitaire, Neuchâtel, Switzerland: "Cet ouvrage dont l'idée fort bonne et qui a d'abord été fort accueilli, est sorti détestable des mains du sot et volumineux abbé de La Porte de manière qu'un grand nombre de personnes qui avaient même les trois premiers volumes [i.e., the two-volume edition of 1769 and the

supplement of 1778] ont refusé d'acquérir le quatrième formé par le supplément."

13   The text of 1784 contains the names of only 1,321 authors, living and dead, as compared with the 1,920 in the supplement of 1778. In order to arrive at a valid estimate of the literary population in 1784, one must go over all the editions and supplements from 1769, counting the authors one by one while weeding out duplicate references and eliminating authors who had died by the end of 1783. The result is 2,819, which I consider a minimal figure.

14   *La France littéraire* provides the only way of measuring the literary population by taking soundings at regular intervals in a homogeneous, contemporary source. I have investigated three other possibilities. The first is *Le [sic] France litéraire [sic] contenant les auteurs françaises [sic] de 1771 à 1796*, 3 vols. (Hamburg, 1797) produced in Germany by J. S. Ersch in 1797. Following an example set forty years earlier by J. H. S. Formey, Ersch compiled references to books and authors from French periodicals, added them to material from the French editions of *La France littéraire* and came up with notices on 4,761 writers scattered through three volumes. But he lumped together everything written between 1771 and 1796, so his work does not reveal much about the number of authors at any specific time. A second and more remarkable survey was conducted by inspector Joseph d'Hémery of the Parisian police between 1748 and 1752. He compiled a dossier on every writer he could locate in the city (also a few outside Paris), reaching a total of 501, a third of the number for the entire kingdom in *La France littéraire* of 1757. I have discussed this survey in "A Police Inspector Sorts His Files: The Anatomy of the Republic of Letters" in *The Great Cat Massacre and Other Episodes in French Cultural History* (New York, 1984), chap. 4, and have published all the reports on my website, Robertdarnton. org. Finally, one could extract statistics from bibliographies and biographical dictionaries such as the catalogue of the Bibliothèque nationale and *Biographie universelle, ancienne et moderne* by Jean-François and Louis-Gabriel Michaud (Paris, 1811–1862). But they contain only spotty information about obscure writers, much of it derived from *La France littéraire*. The most manageable source of this kind is Alexandre Cioranescu's *Bibliographie de la littérature française*

du dix-huitième siècle (Paris, 1969). By sifting it for information about authors alive at the time of the three main soundings in *La France littéraire*, one gets the following results: 1757, 712 writers; 1769, 836 writers; and 1784, 1,017 writers. They confirm the growth from 1769 to 1784, but nearly half the writers have to be eliminated from the count because their dates are unknown.

15 See Pierre Goubert, "Révolution démographique au xviiie siècle?," in *Histoire économique et sociale de la France*, ed. Fernand Braudel and Ernest Labrousse (Paris, 1970), 2:55–84; and Jacques Dupâquier, "Révolution française et révolution démographique," in *Vom Ancien Régime zur französischen Revolution: Forschungen und Perspektiven*, ed. Ernst Hinrichs, Eberhard Schmitt, and Rudolf Vierhaus (Göttingen, 1978), 233–260.

16 German-speaking Europe, which had about the same population, scattered across many political units, as France, had twice as many writers, although not without some Sturm und Drang and a great deal of clamor about the hard lot of authorship: Helmuth Kiesel and Paul Munch, *Gesellschaft und Literatur im 18. Jahrhundert: Voraussetzungen und Entstehung des literarischen Markts in Deutschland* (Munich, 1977), 7–104, esp. at 90, where the number of writers in German-speaking territories is estimated as roughly 3,000 in 1771; 5,200 in 1784; and 6,200 in 1788. These figures are based on J. G. Meusel's *Das gelehrte Teutschland oder Lexicon der letzt lebenden teutschen Schriftsteller* (Leipzig, 1768–1770) and later editions, which seems to have been more thorough in its coverage than *La France littéraire*.

17 Louis-Sébastien Mercier, *Tableau de Paris* (Amsterdam, 1783), 3:107–108.

18 Louis-Sébastien Mercier, *Le Nouveau Paris*, ed. Jean-Claude Bonnet (Paris, 1984), 445–446.

19 Voltaire made these observations in the first of the notes that he wrote in 1771 to accompany his poem, *Le Pauvre Diable*. See *Oeuvres complètes de Voltaire* (Geneva, 1785), 14:164.

20 On the Saint Malo-Genevan line as a demarcation of sociocultural history, see Roger Chartier, "Les Deux Frances: Histoire d'une géographie," *Cahiers d'histoire* (1979), 24:393–415.

21 See, for example, "A Police Inspector Sorts His Files," cited above in note 14.

22 P. F. N. Fabre d'Églantine, *Les Gens de lettres*, published posthumously in *Mélanges littéraires par une société de gens de lettres* (Paris, 1827), 59.

23 Daniel Roche, *Journal de ma vie: Jacques-Louis Ménétra, compagnon vitrier au 18e siècle* (Paris, 1982). The common people probably do not figure in large numbers among the unidentified in the statistics, because they had a *qualité*. If they were artisans, they were identified as such.

3. Contemporary Views

1 Among the works in this literature that are particularly relevant to the following argument, I would cite Jean Le Rond d'Alembert, *Essai sur la société des gens de lettres et des grands, sur la réputation, sur les Mécènes, et sur les récompenses littéraires* in his *Mélanges de littérature, d'histoire et de philosophie* (Amsterdam, 1773, 1st ed. 1752); and Louis Sébastien Mercier, *De la littérature et des littérateurs* (Yverdon, Switzerland, 1778). See also in Mercier's *Tableau de Paris* (Paris, 1789 edition, 12 vols.) the chapters entitled "Auteurs," "Des demi-auteurs, quarts d'auteurs, enfin métis, quarterons," "Misère des auteurs," "La littérature du Faubourg Saint-Germain et celle du Faubourg Saint-Honoré," and "Le Musée de Paris."

2 Fabre's play, performed in 1787, was published posthumously in *Mélanges littéraires par une société de gens de lettres* (Paris, 1827). Rivarol is generally believed to have written *Le Petit Almanach de nos grands hommes* (n.p., 1788) with the collaboration of L.-P.-Q. de Richebourg, marquis of Champcenetz.

3 Quotations from *Le Petit Almanach* can be located easily in the text, under the names of the authors satirized, which appear in alphabetical order.

4 See André Le Breton, *Rivarol, sa vie, ses idées, son talent, d'après des documents nouveaux* (Paris, 1895).

5 *Muses provinciales, ou recueil des meilleures productions du génie des poètes des provinces de France* (Paris, 1788), 88, 213.

6 *Le Pauvre diable* in Voltaire, *Œuvres complètes de Voltaire* (Geneva, 1785), 14:162. The theme appears at many points in Voltaire's works. See, for instance, the entries on "Auteurs," "Charlatan," "Gueux,"

"Mendiants," "Philosophe," and "Quisquis" in his *Dictionnaire philosophique*. He especially stressed the population explosion in Grub Street in "Auteurs": "Cent auteurs compilent pour avoir du pain, et vingt folliculaires font l'extrait, la critique, l'apologie, la satire de ces compilations, dans l'idée d'avoir du pain aussi, parce qu'ils n'ont point de métier. . . . Ces pauvres gens se partagent en deux ou trois bandes, et vont à la quête comme des moines mendiants": *Œuvres complètes*, 52:400–401.

7   Antoine Rivarol, *Petit Dictionnaire des grands hommes de la révolution: Par un Citoyen actif, ci-devant Rien* (Paris, 1790). The remark on Robespierre actually occurred in an article Rivarol wrote for the counterrevolutionary journal *Actes des apôtres* in 1789. It is reprinted in Jean Dutourd, *Rivarol* (Paris, 1963), 186. The entry on Robespierre in the *Petit Dictionnaire* concentrated on his oratory in the National Assembly.

8   *Correspondance littéraire, philosophique et critique par Grimm, Diderot, Raynal, Meister, etc.*, ed. Maurice Tourneux (Paris, 1877–1882), 15:139–142. An equally negative report, compressed into one hostile sentence, appeared in the *Mémoires secrets pour servir à l'histoire de la République des lettres en France* (Paris, 1784–1789) of October 9, 1787. Jean-François La Harpe also noted that the play was "huée d'un bout à l'autre": *Correspondance littéraire adressée à Son Altesse Impériale, Mgr. le Grand-Duc, aujourd'hui Empereur de Russie* (Paris, 1801–1807), 5:386.

9   See the well-documented but hostile biography by Henri d'Alméras, *L'Auteur de: "Il pleut, bergère . . .," Fabre d'Églantine* (Paris, 1906).

10 Fabre d'Églantine, *Les Gens de lettres*, published posthumously in *Mélanges littéraires par une société de gens de lettres* (Paris, 1827), 98.

11 Fabre d'Églantine, *Les Gens de lettres*, 20.

12 Fabre d'Églantine, *Les Gens de lettres*, 69.

13 Fabre d'Églantine, *Les Gens de lettres*, 76–77.

14 For a contemporary key to the characters, see *Correspondance littéraire*, 15:139.

15 Fabre d'Églantine, *Les Gens de lettres*, 65.

16 In a poem written three years earlier, Fabre had attacked the most eminent writers of his time by name and had especially reviled the fashionable philosophes and the Académie française: "Littéraires

tyrans, prêts à tout entreprendre, / Leur cabale renaît sans cesse de sa cendre; / Près d'eux génie, esprit, talents sont superflus; / Du fond de leurs fauteuils ils n'ouvrent qu'aux élus." *L'An 1784, ou l'esprit critique, satire* in *Correspondance de Fabre d'Églantine* (Hamburg, n.d.), 3:196.

17 Fabre d'Églantine, *Les Gens de lettres*, 22–23.

18 See, for example, Fabre d'Églantine, *Les Gens de lettres*, 110 and 115.

19 Fabre d'Églantine, *Les Gens de lettres*, 74–75.

20 Rivarol, *Petit Dictionnaire*, xi.

21 In 1789 rioters hanged their enemies from a lamppost in the Place de Grève, and Desmoulins became known as the author of a pamphlet, *Discourse of the Lamppost to the Parisians*.

22 As in the *Petit Almanach*, all references can be found under the name of the person being discussed, and the names are arranged in alphabetical order.

23 *Petit Almanach*, 52–53.

24 *Petit Almanach*, xi.

25 *Petit Almanach*, vii.

26 *Petit Almanach*, xiii.

27 *Correspondance littéraire*, 15:139–140.

28 *Correspondance littéraire*, 15:214.

29 Fabre d'Églantine, *Le Philinte de Molière, ou la suite du Misanthrope, comédie en cinq actes et en vers* (Paris, 1791), 3, 117.

30 Camille Desmoulins, *Révolutions de France et de Brabant* 3, no. 18 (undated), 127; Jacques-Henri Meister, who had taken over Grimm's *Correspondance littéraire* in 1773 and had less enthusiasm for the Revolution than did Desmoulins, gave a less glowing report of the play's success: *Correspondance littéraire*, 15:595–596. Jean-François La Harpe reported that the play was very well received, despite some lapses in style: La Harpe, *Correspondance littéraire adressée à son Altesse Impériale*, 6:27.

31 Desmoulins, *Révolutions de France*, 131.

32 Desmoulins, *Révolutions de France*, 129.

33 Desmoulins, *Révolutions de France*, 132.

34 Desmoulins, *Révolutions de France*, 127.

35 *Le Philinte de Molière*, 66. The prologue is a dialogue between Acaste and "l'auteur du *Philinte* sous le nom de Damis" (50). By presenting

himself under this name, Fabre emphasized the link between the hero of *Philinte* and the co-hero of *Les Gens de lettres* and identified himself with both of them—that is, playing the part of Alceste as interpreted by Rousseau.

36 *Œuvres de Maximilien Robespierre*, eds. Marc Bouloiseau and Albert Soboul (Paris, 1967), 10:454–455. In a speech to the Jacobins on December 5, 1792, Robespierre denounced Helvétius as follows: "Je ne vois ici que deux hommes dignes de notre hommage, Brutus et J. J. Rousseau. Mirabeau doit tomber, Helvétius doit tomber aussi; Helvétius était un intrigant, un misérable bel esprit, un être immoral, un des plus cruels persécuteurs de ce bon J. J. Rousseau, le plus digne de nos hommages. Si Helvétius avait existé de nos jours, n'allez pas croire qu'il eût embrassé la cause de la liberté: il eût augmenté la foule des intrigants beaux esprits qui désolent aujourd'hui la patrie" (9:143–144).

37 *Œuvres de Robespierre*, 10:455.

38 *Œuvres de Robespierre*, 10:158.

39 *Œuvres de Robespierre*, 10:332.

40 Voltaire, *Candide ou l'optimisme, traduit de l'allemand de Mr le docteur Ralph*, in *Romans et contes* (Paris, 1954), 206.

41 Voltaire, *Candide*, 190.

42 Voltaire, *Candide*, 194.

43 Quoted in Daniel Mornet, *Les Origines intellectuelles de la Révolution française, 1715-1787* (Paris, 1954), 84.

44 It is also the central theme of Voltaire's *Essai sur les moeurs et l'esprit des nations*, which he continuously expanded after its first publication in 1756. But he expressed this theme more effectively and in slightly different form in *Le Siècle de Louis XIV* (1751). For an excellent discussion of *Essai sur les moeurs*, see Antoine Lilti, *L'Héritage des Lumières: Ambivalences de la modernité* (Paris, 2019), chap. 4. I have written a similar interpretation as a "preface" to the eighth and final volume of *Essais sur les moeurs et l'esprit des nations* published by the Voltaire Foundation (Oxford, 2015), xxxi-li.

45 Voltaire, *Le Siècle de Louis XIV* in *Œuvres historiques* (Paris, 1957), 617.

46 Voltaire, *Le Siècle*, 1186.

47 Voltaire, *Le Siècle*, 1012.

48 *Discours sur les sciences et les arts* in Rousseau, *Œuvres complètes* (Paris, 1964), 3:8.

49 On the use of the term "aristocracy of the mind" (*"l'aristocratie de l'esprit"*) during the Revolution, see Morellet, *Mémoires*, 2:30.

4. Careers: Revolutionary Denouements

1   Among the studies of writers, publishing, and literature during the Revolution, see esp. Carla Hesse, *Publishing and Cultural Politics in Revolutionary Paris, 1789–1810* (Berkeley, CA, 1991); *La Révolution du journal 1788–1794*, ed. Pierre Rétat (Paris, 1989); Jeremy Popkin, *Revolutionary News: The Press in France, 1789–1799* (Durham, NC, 1990); *L'Écrivain devant la Révolution*, ed. Jean Sgard (Grenoble, 1990); *La Carmagnole des muses: L'homme de lettres et l'artiste dans la Révolution*, ed. Jean-Claude Bonnet (Paris, 1988); Jean-Claude Bonnet, *Naissance du Panthéon: Essai sur le culte des grands hommes* (Paris, 1998); and Hans-Jürgen Lüsebrink, *L'Adresse à l'Assemblée nationale (31 mai 1791) de Guillaume-Thomas Raynal: Positions, polémiques, répercussions* (Paris, 2018).

2   André Morellet, *Mémoires de l'abbé Morellet de l'Académie française sur le dix-huitième siècle et sur la Révolution*, ed. Jean-Pierre Guicciardi (Paris, 1988), 319.

3   Morellet, *Mémoires*, 379.

4   Morellet, *Mémoires*, 317.

5   Morellet, *Mémoires*, 338.

6   Morellet, *Mémoires*, 323.

7   Michel de Cubières, *Les États-Généraux du Parnasse, de l'Europe, de l'Église, et de Cythère, ou quatre poèmes politiques* (Paris, 1791), 24–26. Writing in a manner as if he were issuing edicts for literature, Cubières proclaimed, "Voulons que la comédie soit populaire" (25). He also noted that thanks to the Revolution, the muses "nous ouvrent au Parnasse une route nouvelle" (53). See Jean-Luc Chappey, "Michel de Cubières et la question du statut d'auteur en révolution," in *L'Insurrection entre histoire et littérature*, ed. Quentin Deluermoz and Anthony Glinder (Paris, 2015), 19-33.

8   Morellet, *Mémoires*, 381.

9   Morellet, *Mémoires*, 346.

10 Morellet, *Mémoires*, 349.

11 Morellet, *Mémoires*, 349.

12 Morellet, *Mémoires*, 353.

13 Morellet, *Mémoires*, 357.

14 Morellet, *Mémoires*, 360.

15 Morellet, *Mémoires*, 364.

16 Quoted in Bertran de la Villehervé, *François-Thomas de Baculard d'Arnaud: Son théatre et ses théories dramatiques* (Paris, 1920), 60.

17 *Les Amants malheureux, ou le comte de Comminges* (The Hague, 1773), quotations from pp. 5 and 49.

18 Quoted in Villehervé, *François-Thomas de Baculard d'Arnaud*, 63.

19 Sébastien-Roch Nicolas known as Chamfort, *Maximes, Pensées, caractères et anecdotes* (Paris, 1796), 260.

20 Baculard d'Arnaud, *Géminvile et Dolimon, ou l'héroisme de l'amour et de l'humanité* (Paris, 1798), 191.

21 Robert L. Dawson, *Baculard d'Arnaud: Life and Prose Fiction* (Banbury, UK, 1976), 608. On d'Arnaud's poverty during the Revolution, see also Charles Monselet, *Les Originaux du siècle dernier: Les oubliés et les dédaignés* (Paris, 1864), 305–316.

22 Villehervé, *François-Thomas de Baculard d'Arnaud*, 42.

23 *Les Lettres de P. Manuel, l'un des administrateurs de 1789, sur la Révolution, recueillies par un ami de la constitution* (Paris, n.d. [1792]), 98.

24 *Vie secrète de Pierre Manuel* (Paris, 1793), 47. Although it is the only source of information about many details of Manuel's early life, the *Vie secrète* was a hostile libel, which must be read with skepticism. Manuel himself published several documents in *Les Lettres de P. Manuel*, which include the first of the many speeches he delivered— an exhortation to the combined districts of Val-de-Grâce and Saint Jacques on August 10, 1789, about the need to provide more members for the National Guard (71).

25 *Interrogatoire de Pierre Manuel, Procureur de la Commune* (n.p. n.d. [1792]), 14.

26 *Actes de la Commune de Paris pendant la Révolution française*, ed. Sigismond Lacroix (Paris, 1894), 1st ser., 2:682. In *La Bastille dévoilée, ou Recueil de pièces authentiques pour servir à son histoire* (Paris, 1790), Manuel described himself as "conseiller administrateur au département de la police" (7:151). On the reorganization of the municipal government, see Paul Robiquet, *Le Personnel municipal*

de Paris pendant la Révolution (Paris, 1890), which mentions Manuel (253–254).

27   In proclaiming the freedom of expression, Article 11 of the Declaration ended with the proviso "sauf à répondre à l'abus de cette liberté dans les cas déterminés par la loi." During the next two years, conservatives would invoke that proviso in order to limit what they took to be the excessive license of the radical press.

28   *Les Lettres de P. Manuel*, 141. See also in that collection "Lettre à un censeur royal sur la liberté de la presse" (90–98) and an open letter to Camille Desmoulins (111), both undated.

29   Although *La Bastille dévoilée* appeared anonymously, Manuel did not hide his authorship of it, and he put his name on the title page of *La Police de Paris dévoilée*. He did not acknowledge his authorship of the more scabrous *La Chasteté du clergé dévoilée*, which, however, appeared as a sequel to the first two and resembles them in its character and style.

30   Manuel explained his position in 1792 during a trial that concerned the publication of Mirabeau's letters: *Interrogatoire de Pierre Manuel, Procureur de la Commune* (n.p., 1792), 7–8. The quotations come from *La Bastille dévoilée, ou recueil de pièces authentiques pour servir à son histoire* (Paris, 1789), 1:2–3; and 6:2. Although Manuel claimed that proceeds from the sale of *La Bastille dévoilée* would go to the widows of the Bastille's conquerors, it is unlikely that any payments were made.

31   *Mercure de France*, Dec. 19, 1789; and Jan. 16, 1790.

32   In describing his way of working in the later installments, Manuel stressed "le nombre infini de recherches qu'il faut faire, de pièces qu'il faut rassembler, compulser; de mémoires, de brochures quelquefois ignorées qu'il faut recouvrir, consulter. . . . Pour le même prisonnier il faut quelquefois avoir affaire à vingt personnes différentes." *La Bastille dévoilée*, 5:1.

33   *La Bastille dévoilée*, 3:75 and 105; and Jacques-Pierre Brissot, *Mémoires (1754–1793)*, ed. Claude Perroud (Paris, 1910), 2:23.

34   *La Bastille dévoilée*, 7:126.

35   *Mémoires historiques et authentiques sur la Bastille* (London, 1789). In a "Discours préliminaire," Carra developed a sales pitch and an indignant rhetoric similar to Manuel's. He enticed his readers as follows:

"Lisez et vous frémirez d'indignation et vous jouirez pleinement de l'humiliation des tyrans" (vi).

36 See *La Bastille dévoilée*, 4:3–4. Carra may have abandoned his publication, because at the end of 1789, he took up a career as a journalist on *Annales patriotiques et littéraires*.

37 *La Bastille dévoilee*, 5:2. Manuel warned the reader about misinterpreting the material he published as sheer sensationalism (4:144): "Ce n'est point la satire des personnes renfermées à la Bastille que l'on a l'intention de faire, c'est le tableau des maux qu'ils y ont soufferts, c'est l'histoire des abus commis pendant longtemps en France par toutes les personnes chargées d'une plus ou moins grande portion de l'autorité." But he also stressed its sensationalist appeal as "une galerie morale et animée, aussi piquante pour les contemporains qu'instructive et curieuse pour la postérité" (7:15).

38 *La Bastille dévoilee*, 5:143.

39 *La Police de Paris devoilée* (Paris, 1790), 2:140.

40 *La Chronique scandaleuse, ou mémoires pour servir à l'histoire de la génération présente, contenant les anecdotes et les pièces fugitives les plus piquantes que l'histoire secrète des sociètés a offertes pendant ces dernières années*, vol. 5, 4th ed. (Paris, 1791), preface and pp. 5 and 36.

41 *La Police de Paris dévoilée*, 2:229.

42 *La Police de Paris dévoilée*, 1:321 and 2:87.

43 *Mercure*, July 23, 1791.

44 *La Chasteté du clergé dévoilée, ou procès-verbaux des séances du clergé chez les filles de Paris, trouvés à la Bastille* (Paris, 1790), x.

45 After describing a Franciscan monk caught naked with two prostitutes, the editor regretted that the scene was not accompanied by an illustration, "mais l'imagination du lecteur peut y suppléer" (1:24).

46 *Vie secrète de Pierre Manuel*, 47–49. In a somewhat confused account of the book's origin, the *Vie secrète* also noted that Manuel had sold some of the manuscripts to the Parisian publisher Pierre Duplain. It therefore seems possible that Duplain might have produced *La Chasteté du clergé dévoilée.*

47 On Mirabeau and the controversy connected with the *Lettres originales de Mirabeau*, see Louis de Loménie, *Les Mirabeau* (Paris, 1889), 3:313–326.

48 *Lettres originales de Mirabeau, écrites du donjon de Vincennes pendant les années 1777, 78, 79 et 80: Contenant tous les détails sur sa vie privée, ses malheurs, et ses amours avec Sophie Ruffei, marquise de Monnier recueillies par P. Manuel, citoyen français* (Paris, 1792), quotations from pp. xvi, xvii, 14, and 16. Manuel celebrated his role as editor of the letters: "J'ai tout recueilli, tout rapproché: ces débris de l'amour étaient pour moi des reliques, et mon coeur a suppléé à mes yeux. Eh! n'avais-je pas grand besoin, moi qui ai eu la peine de publier le *Livre rouge* de la vice [that is, *La Police de Paris dévoilée*], de rédiger, pour rafraichir mon sang, les mémoires de ce héros de Vincennes" (ix).

49 *Lettres originales de Mirabeau*, quotations from 1:29, 31, 32, 45, 46, 49. In fact, as Loménie explained, the lovers had two correspondences, one of which was in code and contained the most erotic language.

50 Chénier's letter appeared in the *Journal de Paris* of February 12, 1792, and is reprinted in André Chénier, *Œuvres complètes*, ed. Gérard Walter (Paris, 1950), 267–272.

51 *Interrogatoire de Pierre Manuel, procureur de la Commune* (1792). Manuel argued that the book "devait faire le plus grand honneur à Mirabeau, et en vengeant le fondateur de la liberté inspirer une horreur éternelle pour le despotisme" (9).

52 *Interrogatoire de Pierre Manuel*, 14.

53 On the affair of the Mirabeau letters, see the documents in *Actes de la Commune de Paris pendant la Révolution française*, ed. Sigismond Lacroix, 2nd ser. (Paris, 1894), 8:551–608.

54 *Les Lettres de Pierre Manuel, l'un des administrateurs de 1789, sur la Révolution, recueillies par un ami de la constitution* (Paris, 1792), quotations from pp. iv, 16, 115.

55 *Discours sur la guerre prononcé aux Amis de la constitution par Pierre Manuel* (1792) and F. A. Aulard, *La Société des Jacobins. Recueil de documents pour l'histoire du Club des Jacobins* (Paris, 1897), 3:348.

56 Aulard, *La Société des Jacobins*, 3:267, 335, 348, 364, and 374.

57 *Résumé pour Charles-Pierre Bosquillon, citoyen actif, contre M. Manuel, élu procureur de la Commune de Paris* (Paris, 1791), quotation from p. 11.

58 Aulard, *La Société des Jacobins*, 3:364.

59 Aulard, *La Société des Jacobins*, 4:111. See also Paul Robiquet, *Le Personnel municipal de Paris pendant la Révolution* (Paris, 1890), 488–498.

60 Louis Sébastien Mercier, *Le Nouveau Paris*, ed. Jean-Claude Bonnet (Paris, 2004), 445–447.

61 Aulard, *La Société des Jacobins*, 4:460.

62 Germaine de Staël, *Considérations sur la Révolution française*, ed. Jacques Godechot (Paris, 1983), 283–286. According to another contemporary account, Manuel bravely saved several lives during the massacres: *Mémoires et notes de Choudieu*, ed. Victor Barrucand (Paris, 1897), 204.

63 *Opinion de P. Manuel sur la première question: pour le jugement de Louis XVI* (Paris, 1792).

64 On Manuel's role in the king's trial, see *Jugement rendu par le Tribunal révolutionnaire, établi par la loi du 10 mars 1793, séant à Paris au Palais, qui … condamne Pierre Manuel à la peine de mort, conformément à la loi du 16 décembre 1792* (Paris, 24 brumaire, An II) and *Réimpression de l'ancien Moniteur* 18 (Paris, 1860), issue for November 16, 1793.

65 On Manuel's last days, see the works cited in the previous note and *Vie secrète de Pierre Manuel*, which has information from sources in Montargis, although, as mentioned, it must be read with skepticism. The *Véritable Testament de Pierre Manuel, ci-devant procureur de la Commune et député à la Convention nationale, écrit la veille de sa mort dans la prison de la Conciergerie, suivi de plusieurs morales touchantes qu'il fit au Tribunal révolutionnaire pour gagner le peuple à son avantage* (n.p., n.d.) is equally tendentious.

Conclusion

1 See my *Pirating and Publishing: The Book Trade in the Age of Enlightenment* (New York, 2021).

2 In *A Field of Honor: Writers, Court Culture and Public Theater in French Literary Life from Racine to the Revolution* (New York, 2002), Gregory S. Brown argues convincingly that the notorious victimization of playwrights by the actors of the Comédie française, which led to Beaumarchais's Société des auteurs dramatiques in 1777, was more about the status and dignity of the authors than income from the box office.

3   *Conseils d'un vieil auteur à un jeune, ou l'art de parvenir dans la République des lettres* (London, 1758), attributed to André-Hyacinthe Sabatier, quotations from pp. 7, 10, and 14.

4   Paul Bénichou, *Le Sacre de l'écrivain (1750–1780): Essai sur l'avènement d'un pouvoir spirituel laïque dans la France moderne* (Paris, 1973). Although Bénichou formally ends his study in 1780, he devotes most of it to the nineteenth century.

5   See Jean-Claude Bonnet, *Naissance du Panthéon: Essai sur le culte des grands hommes* (Paris, 1998); and Roger Chartier, *The Cultural Origins of the French Revolution* (Durham, NC, 1991).

ACKNOWLEDGMENTS

By concentrating on writers, this book closes a cycle of works I have written on publishers, pirates, booksellers, censors, underground literature, and the distribution of books in eighteenth-century France. To acknowledge everyone who has helped me since I began this research in 1965 would be to write yet another volume. But I cannot end this one without thanking Harvard University Press, which published my first book in 1968 and is now publishing my last. I also would like to express my gratitude to the Paris Institute for Advanced Study, which invited me to spend a month in 2024 revising arguments from my early work, as I explain in the introduction to this book. Susan Karani Virtanen did excellent work in editing the manuscript at Harvard University Press, and Sharmila Sen, the editorial director of the press, kindly hastened its journey to publication. Finally, I owe a great debt to Éric Vigne, my editor at Éditions Gallimard, who helped me revise the text before I submitted it for translation into French.

INDEX